F⊙RENSIC
CASE FILES

THE

Diagnosing and Treating the Pathologies
of the American Health System

THE FORENSIC CASE FILES

Diagnosing and Treating the Pathologies of the American Health System

David Barton Smith

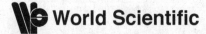

World Scientific

NEW JERSEY · LONDON · SINGAPORE · BEIJING · SHANGHAI · HONG KONG · TAIPEI · CHENNAI

Published by

World Scientific Publishing Co. Pte. Ltd.

5 Toh Tuck Link, Singapore 596224

USA office: 27 Warren Street, Suite 401-402, Hackensack, NJ 07601

UK office: 57 Shelton Street, Covent Garden, London WC2H 9HE

British Library Cataloguing-in-Publication Data
A catalogue record for this book is available from the British Library.

THE FORENSIC CASE FILES
Diagnosing and Treating the Pathologies of the American Health System

ISBN-13 978-981-283-837-7
ISBN-10 981-283-837-6

Typeset by Stallion Press
Email: enquiries@stallionpress.com

Printed in Singapore.

Dedication

To my students who have been my teachers

Preface

As this book goes to press, the pathologies of the American health system and the prescriptions for their treatment are the focus of a heated national debate and pending legislation. The cases presented in this book provide stark, concrete examples of the underlying barriers that make healthcare reform so essential yet frustratingly difficult. These barriers include how the American healthcare system is governed, its physicians organized, nursing care provided, its services paid for, its market works and how all of it is regulated.

I started writing *The Forensic Case Files* with the aim to assist those within the United States healthcare system in understanding the underlying problems so they could address them. It became clear that they need a lot of help. I ended up writing for a broader audience for two reasons.

First, the American public owns their health system. They own it through the taxes they pay, the benefits they purchase through employment and the special tax exemptions and subsidies they provide to assure decent care. It is not owned by private insurance plans, hospital chains, or pharmaceutical corporations any more than the armed forces are owned by defense contractors. The special dispensations to non-profit "private" health plans and health systems make them an arm of the state, in essence owned by the public. The issue is not about "government takeovers" or a battle to preserve "free markets." The issue is how the American public wants to govern their health system. Its pathologies result from the absentee ownership vacuum that has been filled by special interests. It is time the public owners stopped being absentee ones.

Second, the public owners of the health system must now ask a critical moral question. Should everyone just take care of themselves or should we look after each other? Most Americans would lean towards the "we should look after each other" answer to this question but how this should be done is the focus of the current debate. Most of the cases in this book describe the troubling consequences of private market approaches to "taking care of each other" that too few have paid attention to.

Writing the cases in this book about the pathologies in the American health system was both exhilarating and uncomfortable. The stories had twists and turns that I had never thought about before. It was also an opportunity, with the unique freedom only afforded at the end of one's career, to tell the truth about the most complex, troubling and intractable problem faced in the United States. Yet, it was difficult to find a balance between the admiration and affection I feel for those who work in healthcare and the discouraging pathologies of the system within which they work. In some of the revelations in this book I felt I was being disloyal. I can only hope that the effort to reveal the truth is the ultimate form of loyalty and the path to correction of the pathologies, but it is uncomfortable.

I have accumulated a lot of debts in pulling these stories together. The result is a collective distillation of so many people that it is impossible to acknowledge them all here. While the flaws are mine alone, whatever redeeming values this book has is a reflection of their collective influence.

The more than 1,000 students in healthcare careers that I have worked with in the Cornell University Sloan Program in Healthcare Management, the University of Rochester Community Medicine Department, the Healthcare Management program in the business school at Temple University and in the Drexel University School of Public Health have served as my teachers and sources of many of the pieces of the stories presented here. They are acknowledged in the dedication of this book. I hope that their efforts to educate me, as reflected in the cases in this book, will be of assistance to those now entering healthcare careers.

Colleagues have played a critical role in shaping the ideas in this book. These include Roger Battistella and John Kuder at Cornell, William Barker, Ernest Saward and Bob Berg at the University of Rochester Community Medicine Department, and long time friend and co-author Arnold Kaluzny at the Cecil G. Sheps Center for Health Services Research at the University of North Carolina. I am deeply indebted to my colleagues at Temple University, particularly those in the Risk, Insurance and Healthcare Management Department, Bill Aaronson, Tom Getzen, Chuck Hall and Jacqueline Zinn where I spent the bulk of my career. More recent collaborators have included Dennis Andrulis at the Drexel University School of Public Health's Center for Health Equality, Zhanlian Feng, Vince Mor and Mary Fennell at the Center for Gerontology and Health Services Research at Brown University and Mary Jane Koren at the Commonwealth Fund. Early influences included a remarkable group of pioneering researchers and healthcare reformers who guided me as a doctoral student in The University of Michigan's program in Medical Organization — Solomon J. Axelrod, Avedis Donabedian, Gene Feingold and Charles Metzner.

This book provided the opportunity to revisit joint efforts of the past to which many contributed. These included a book on the regulation of nursing homes supported by a grant from what is now the Agency for Healthcare Research and Quality and published by Health Administration Press, a book on the racial integration of healthcare supported by a grant from the Robert Wood Johnson Foundation and published by The University of Michigan Press, work on allied health workforce supply and demand in the Philadelphia area and in Pennsylvania supported by the Pennsylvania Center for Health Careers of the Workforce Investment Board with the assistance of Bill Aaronson at Temple University and a health assessment for the Pottstown Health and Wellness Foundation done in collaboration with DGA Partners, with the assistance of John Harris. I am also indebted to the Temple University Heart Transplant Team, particularly Jack Kolff, director of the program at the time and the Gift of Life Donor Program and its director Howard Nathan for their assistance in providing me the opportunity to observe and learn from their efforts.

Investigative reporters and the newspapers that support them troll the same waters as academic researchers but are so much better at catching the big fish and providing the richness in detail. I am indebted, as we all are to their efforts, so critical for a democracy. Two such talented efforts were particularly helpful in fleshing out several of the cases in this book: Steve Massey's series in the *Pittsburgh Post-Gazette* on the AHERF bankruptcy and John Shiftman's series in the *Philadelphia Inquirer* on the investigation of Akhil Bansal's illegal internet prescription network.

In helping with the heavy lifting in preparing this manuscript, I am indebted to many. Dennis Andrulis, Richie Kahn, Ray Lum, Robert Pickard and Jonathan Purtle at Drexel University's School of Public Health provided very helpful comments on portions of the manuscript. Judy Harrington, Vice President at Health Partners provided a particularly useful guidance on the AHERF and HealthChoices cases. Long time friend and colleague Bob Uris crafted the U.S. Healthcare case. I am particularly indebted to a comprehensive review by Joel Telles, Systems Director, Data Management and Analysis at Main Line Health on the entire manuscript. All of his thoughtful suggestions were not possible to include in this manuscript but perhaps several new books will be in the offing. Granddaughter Shannon Eaton, sociologist in training at the University of Maryland, provided encouragement and useful suggestions. I am deeply grateful to Mary Ellen Cook at the Center for Health Equality at Drexel who added to her many duties the tracking down of permissions. I am also indebted to Deborah Ruth Hoffman of Swarthmore who with a very tight deadline expertly handled the initial editing of a very rough manuscript before it was sent to the publisher. On the other side of the world, V.K. Sanjeed of Singapore also expertly handled the editing and final proof preparation for World Scientific Publishing.

As with previous books, my wife, Joan K. Apt reviewed all the chapters and assisted with the preparation of the index with the useful commentary of an experienced and skeptical healthcare manager but supportive helpmate. I have indeed been fortunate. I can only hope that our youngest son, Alex, now entering the doctoral program in Economics at the University of Virginia will be as fortunate.

Contents

1

Introduction: Fixing Healthcare in the United States

Pamela Davis, CEO of 427 bed Edward Hospital in Naperville, Illinois was instructed by the FBI to wear a wire in her bra to collect evidence of a shakedown that had held up the state health planning approval of a hospital expansion. That investigation initiated by Davis eventually led to the uncovering of then Governor Blagojevitch's efforts to sell President Obama's Senate seat. The hospital expansion has yet to be approved (Burleigh, 2009).

A multinational corporation, Siemens, whose subsidiaries include Siemens Healthcare, this nation's largest vendor of computerized medical information systems for hospitals and office practices, agreed to pay $1.6 billion in fines to settle charges that it routinely used bribes to gain contracts on every continent on the globe. The annual budget for bribes, which according to the New York Times account "was just a line item," was about $40 to $50 million a year (Schubert and Miller, 2008). Indeed, it was such an accepted operating procedure within the corporation, that it was routinely reported as a business expense. Up until 1999, such expenses were a legitimate deductible business expense under the German tax code.

Schools that train the people who work in healthcare do not cover this aspect of the industry. Those involved in these events rarely discuss them openly. They are part of a dark underside of professional life that is not unique to the health sector. There is a large gray area between the bribery engaged in by Siemens executives and the extortion attempt faced by Pamela Davis and the ideals that shape professional codes of ethics. There is an even larger gap between how well healthcare in the United States performs and how well it could. How do we fix this? In essence, we can begin to fix it by learning from history, mistakes and a growing appreciation of the complex interconnectedness of the U.S. health system. This book helps by presenting cases that contain three common elements: (1) a history that places the case in the context of the evolution of healthcare in the United States, (2) serious ethical lapses or mistakes and (3) concrete examples of that interconnectedness. Taken together, the cases make a compelling argument for both the necessity and capacity for corrective treatment.

Whether you are a nurse or doctor in training, a lawyer involved in representing a client, a manager in a healthcare plan, hospital or clinic, a regulator, an interest group lobbyist, a legislator concerned about influencing policy, or a patient or relative of a patient trying to ensure the provision of adequate care, there are lots of troubling surprises.

In the United States, as in other countries, health is our most precious national resource. It is essential for our individual "pursuit of happiness" as embodied in our Declaration of Independence. As a nation, it helps determine our productivity, our ability to compete in the global marketplace, our military capacity to defend ourselves and our credibility in world affairs. We regularly take stock of how we are doing relative to other countries and the numbers trouble us.

We certainly spend enough money. We spent more per person — $6,401 per capita in 2005 — representing a higher percent of our gross domestic product (15.3%) than any other nation in the world (Organization for Economic Cooperation and Development (OECD), 2007). The United States now spends more than $2 trillion dollars on healthcare, exceeding the total Gross Domestic Product (GDP) of all the other 30 developed countries providing information except Japan. It accounts for close to a staggering *half* of all the health expenditures in the world. While we are the only one of these 30 developed nations that lacks a system of assuring universal health insurance coverage for all its citizens, we still spend more in public dollars alone per capita for healthcare ($3,041 in 2005) than the

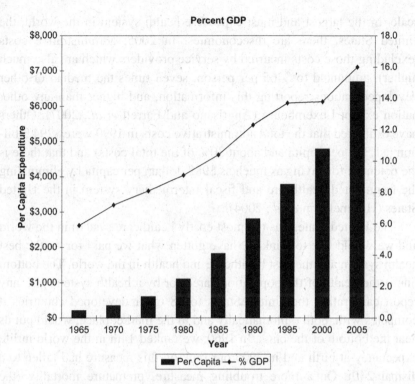

Fig. 1.1. U.S. Per Capita Health Expenditures and Percent of Gross Domestic Product 1965–2005 (*Source*: CMS, Office of the Actuary, 2007).

average *total* per capita expenditures for healthcare in all of these countries. As indicated in Fig. 1.1, those expenditures continue to rise at a rapid rate with no end in sight. If health expenditures were to continue to rise at roughly the same rate as they have over the last 40 years, healthcare would devour more than 40% of our Gross Domestic Product in 2045. If that pattern were to continue another forty years after that, national expenditures would exceed the entire GDP creating an implausible science fiction world where it would be impossible to sustain life — ironically the very purpose of these expenditures.

Almost as troubling, we spend a substantially larger share of our healthcare costs, not on providing healthcare services, but on trying to manage them. In large businesses, there are administrative economies of scale. In the largest and most expensive health system in the world, the United States, there are diseconomies. In 2005, administrative costs (excluding those costs incurred by service providers which are also much higher), amounted to $465 per person, seven times the median of other developed nations reporting this information, and higher than any other nation except Luxembourg (Angrisano and Farrell *et al.*, 2007). Others have estimated that the total administrative costs in 1999 were $294.3 billion ($1,389 per capita and about 30% of the total costs) and that there is the potential for saving as much as $982 dollars per capita by eliminating the fragmented healthcare and fiscal intermediary system in the United States (Himmelstein *et al.*, 2004).

The United States has the most costly healthcare system in the world and we would like to think we have gotten what we paid for — the best health system and the best healthcare and health in the world. The bottom line is the health of the population cared for by a health system. Yet, any report card rating the United States to 28 other developed countries it competes with, both diplomatically and in the market place, would put us near the bottom of the class. In 1960, we ranked 14th in the world in life expectancy at birth and in 2005 our rank on this measure had fallen to a dismal 24th. On a more troubling measure, premature mortality (the potential years of life lost before age seventy due to deaths before this age), the United States ranks 27th for women and 24th for men among these 28 nations. A combination of higher rates of infant mortality, homicide and death from accidents contribute to this poor showing. In general, the amount of money expended per capita on healthcare correlates with better health and life expectancy. As noted in Fig. 1.2, however, the United States is the lonely outlier, spending more and getting much less in return.

We are quite defensive about these statistics and try to dismiss them. Some argue, it is not the fault of our health system — rather it is people's lifestyles and personal behavior, together with social and economic problems beyond the responsibility of healthcare providers, that produce these poor results. This is certainly a part of the problem and it is interwoven into many of the cases in this book. Others would argue that we provide the access to services that Americans demand, whereas the publicly dominated financing mechanisms in these other countries ration services in

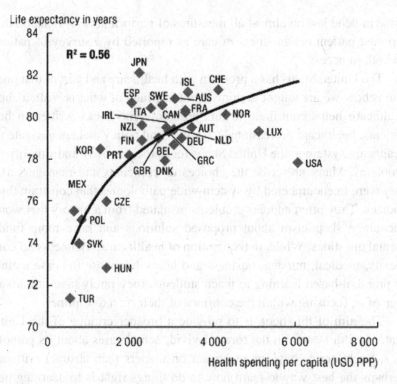

Fig. 1.2. Life Expectancy at Birth and Per Capita Health Expenditures (*Source*: OECD, 2007).

a way that Americans would not tolerate and this accounts for the higher cost. However, at least in terms of supply of physicians, nurses and hospital beds, which are crude measures of ease of access, we are well below the average for these developed countries. Indeed, on average, citizens of these other countries receive *more* services in terms of both physician visits per year and admissions to hospitals per year than Americans. Others argue that Americans like the kind of responsiveness of the care they get, while citizens of other countries are unhappy with the "rigidity of government controlled" systems of care. The Commonwealth Fund conducted a detailed study, including surveys of physicians and the population as a whole ranking the performance of the health systems of six countries (Australia, Canada, Germany, New Zealand, the United Kingdom, and the United States) (Davis, Schoen *et al.*, 2007). The United States health system came in dead last on almost all measures of performance. It ranked 5th in reported patient centeredness of care as reported by a survey of patients and 6th in access.

The United States has a problem with healthcare and part of that problem is how we are taught to think about it. Much of what is written about healthcare helps contribute to this problem. The books written to help patients, healthcare professionals, lawyers and policy makers navigate the healthcare system in the United States focus too narrowly and simplify the problems. Many prescribe the choices of clinicians and managers as if they were unencumbered by system-wide pathologies that constrain those choices. They often address problems insulated from a history that would encourage skepticism about proposed solutions and raise more fundamental questions. While, in recognition of health care's richness and complexity, medical, nursing, business and law schools use the case method or problem-based learning to teach students, they rarely take full advantage of it, focusing within the confines of their own discipline.

The aim of this book is to provide a broader critique of the United States health system in the form of vivid, actual cases about its pathologies. Such stories have more impact on readers than abstract critiques. Perhaps the best way to learn how to do things right is by learning how wrong things can go. The cases that follow involve the more substantive stories, those buried beneath headlines and the casual retelling of personal frustrations by those who work or receive care in health settings. They involve sometimes Byzantine intrigues that have shaped the widening disparities in treatment, escalating costs, unsafe and inadequate care for patients, and the growing demoralization of the many decent and committed people who work within the system.

While each of the cases could be read separately, together they address most of the basic structural problems faced by healthcare in the United States. These include the problems of: (1) ownership and governance, (2) the limitation of existing mechanisms of quality control, (3) the cyclical shortages of nursing staff and other providers of care, (4) the failure of government controls to regulate healthcare or to eliminate racial and ethnic disparities in treatment, (5) the failure of market forces to address the escalating cost and fragmentation of care, and (6) the political barriers to effective collaboration toward improving the health of communities.

Each case will be introduced with a preface that explains how the case fits with the others and into the evolution of the health system in the United States. Where appropriate, a postscript will bring the issues illustrated in the case up to date.

The book will be of interest to the general reader, but is designed to serve as a companion text to introductory courses in health management and policy for students in sociology, political science, public health, medicine, management, allied health, and law.

I wanted to provide a readable book with plenty of interesting stories. The stories are not typical of what happens in healthcare settings on a day to day basis. They are stories where people involved in the provision of healthcare find themselves pushed into a grey area, raising professional, ethical, legal, and sometimes criminal questions.

I wanted, however, to do more than just provide entertaining stories about the ethical dilemmas faced by those organizing, financing and delivering healthcare. I wanted to provide an antidote to approaches to healthcare that rob it of its complexity, historical ironies and human drama that make the healthcare setting such an interesting place to work. The cases or stories in this book raise fundamental questions not just about healthcare, but about who we are, how we should live our lives and what we should strive to be as communities and as a nation in an ever more interconnected world.

The fundamental lesson of these stories is that, while healthcare in the United States has profound pathologies, we also have the capacity to address them. In an academic health center, patients dread when the doctors providing care really get interested in their case, and bring in their students to learn and colleagues to consult. It is surely a sign that they have a complex and potentially fatal illness. Yet, through marshalling all the best of what we know, all the best of our resources and all the best of our intentions, it may be one that is possible to cure. That same combination of dread, fascination and hope draws people to healthcare and is woven through the cases in this book.

2

Governance: Who's in Charge?

Organizing the Owners

Who owns healthcare in the United States and how is accountability to those owners assured? Eyes glaze over when you talk about ownership. What everyone in the United States takes for granted mystifies those from other countries. Yet, we have trouble explaining it and the more we talk about it, the more confused we become. Unlike in most other developed countries, the bulk of the physical plant and capital resources in the United States are owned by non-profit voluntary organizations that are neither publicly nor privately owned. For example, of all the non-federal general acute hospital beds in the United States, which account for most of healthcare's capital resources, 14% are in privately owned for profit facilities, 16% are owned by state and local governments and the remaining 70% are owned by non-profit or voluntary organizations (National Center for Health Statistics, 2007, pp. 364). The money to pay for the construction of these facilities mostly comes from the accumulated equity or profits and debt in the form of mortgages or bonds. In addition, voluntary facilities obtain money to pay for such construction from charitable endowments; public facilities may get money from taxes and for profit operations from stock offerings.

Even the regulation of hospitals in the United States, something that governments are supposed to do to assure the safety and efficacy of the care the public receives, has been largely delegated to voluntary

9

organizations. For example, the Joint Commission determines which hospitals meet standards of quality and are eligible to receive government Medicare reimbursement. The Joint Commission is a non-profit organization with board representation from all of the major national hospital and medical profession trade associations. Within an individual hospital, a voluntary medical staff organization has the primary responsibility for determining which doctors will be allowed the privilege of admitting patients, what procedures they are sufficiently qualified to perform, and then monitoring their performance and the overall quality of care within the hospital.

The majority of hospitals in the United States and the way all hospital care is regulated are part of a "third way," voluntarism or professionalism, neither truly government or privately owned. The approach fits the recently evolved political theory of "Communitarianism," that tries to split the differences between socialists and free market conservatives by proposing a "civil society" populated by non-governmental organizations that enrich people's lives and meet the human needs of the less fortunate among us. The underlying question, of course, is the same: who controls or owns these organizations, whose interests do they really represent and what do they do with them as a consequence?

Most of the money to pay for hospital services, 56.8%, flows from public sources, namely Medicare and Medicaid (National Center for Health Statistics, 2007, pp. 397). Only 3.3% of hospital services are paid for out of the patients' pockets and the rest of the money flows from private insurance plans largely acquired through employer based coverage. This hotly contested market is roughly evenly distributed between historically voluntary or non-profit plans (Blue Cross/Blue Shield and others) and commercial insurance companies. One would think that real ownership or control would flow from the source of the money used to pay for these facilities. This, however, is not the case.

Why is healthcare owned largely by voluntary organizations? Is one form of ownership really "better" than another? A lot of effort has been invested in trying to answer this question. At least on the surface, for acute care hospitals, it does not seem to make much of a difference. Few have found significant ownership differences in the quality of care or the efficiency of operations (Stone, 2008). In the same regulatory and financing environments, they all behave pretty much the same way and produce pretty much the same results.

We have always been ambivalent about the ownership question. As a country largely settled by immigrants trying to escape from what they regarded as oppressive government control of their lives, we have an aversion to government ownership. Yet, modern medicine and hospitals in the United States emerged out of healthcare reform efforts, not to liberate healthcare from government control, but to curb abuses of the private free market in the 19th and early 20th century. During this period, a person could practice medicine with a mail order degree from a for-profit degree mill and charlatan commercial enterprises peddled patent medicines whose only active ingredient was either alcohol or opium. Hospitals that were privately owned by physicians lacked any independent controls over quality and the appropriateness of the procedures these physician-owners engaged in. Some just did a lot of unnecessary, but profitable surgery. A few were incompetent butcher shops. The stigma that some of these facilities left still lingers over privately owned hospitals today.

Most of the older hospitals in the United Sates were originally established as charities. They were viewed as places of last resort for patients who lacked the resources and family support to be cared for in their own homes. Until around 1910, most did not even consider collecting money from their patients. Those who could afford to pay would have gotten better care at home and would not have thought of entering facilities serving the indigent who had no other choice. Today, most of these same charitable or voluntary hospitals provide care almost exclusively for paying patients and some have developed sophisticated strategies for limiting the small amount of charitable care they provide for the poor.

In part, ownership patterns are a legacy of the settlement and development of the United States. The Northeast and the Midwest, where most of the older cities and wealth was concentrated, have a higher proportion of voluntary facilities and the West and South more for-profit facilities.

However, this is not the whole story. Hospitals can change their ownership status. Public hospitals convert to voluntary ones, voluntary ones are sold to proprietary chains and proprietary chains sell hospitals back to voluntary organizations in local communities. Yet, the overall mix and dominance of voluntary ownership has remained essentially unchanged for one hundred years.

In essence, voluntary ownership persists as the dominant form because most hospital managers and physicians prefer it. Voluntary ownership gives them more autonomy and flexibility. This is what professionals expect and what is usually expected of them. The public willingness to delegate a large degree of autonomy to physicians and voluntary healthcare organizations stems from both the perception that they know a lot more than we do and that they will place the needs of their patients and the communities they serve ahead of their own self interests. Professionals and professional organizations are not directly accountable to the public. Nor are they constrained by quarterly performance requirements, the way publicly traded corporations are. Voluntary ownership provides managers and doctors with more slack. Healthcare managers and doctors — like everyone else — do not like to have what they do controlled by others. In a voluntary organization, the medical staff, along with the facility managers, have more room to chart their own course. They are constrained only by how the organization is governed and both management and the medical staff are represented on the board responsible for charting its course. Most of the boards of voluntary healthcare organizations use this extra flexibility to better serve their patients and communities.

The leadership of some voluntary hospitals, however, assume that they have almost unlimited freedom to steer the organization anywhere they choose and their obligations to the communities they serve become confused with their own self interests. This is evident in the two cases presented in this chapter. In Case 1 (HealthEast), the hospital was stopped short by the legal constraints of their charter as a tax-exempt charity and the displeasure of their community. In Case 2 (Allegheny Health, Education and Research Foundation (AHERF)), the health system crashed and burned, a disastrous victim of it's own financial recklessness in an unforgiving environment.

Case 1: HealthEast and the Misplaced Mission of a Voluntary System

Allentown
Well we're living here in Allentown
And they're closing all the factories down
Out in Bethlehem they're killing time
Filling out forms
Standing in line.
(*Billy Joel, 1982*).

Background

Most people in Allentown liked Billy Joel's 1982 song about their then struggling, gritty, blue collar town. The mayor awarded a key to the city to Billy Joel shortly after its release. Allentown, the place where the Liberty Bell was hidden during the British occupation of Philadelphia in the War for Independence, serves as a metaphor for the heartland of the nation. Widespread manufacturing layoffs built a culture of distrust that produced a bumpy ride for efforts to transform the voluntary hospitals in the region.

The first attempt began with an ambitious effort in the 1960s to combine the city's two largest hospitals, Sacred Heart, a Catholic facility and Allentown Hospital, a non-denominational facility. The merger's fate was chronicled in a series of articles, "The Hospital Memoirs" in Allentown's paper, *The Morning Call* (Fleishman and Wlazelek, 1987). The plan was to create under one roof a new "super" regional medical center, Allentown Sacred Heart Medical Center (ASH). It had intuitive appeal, particularly during the height of efforts to develop regional plans for hospital services locally and nationally. The two landlocked older facilities would get a new state of the art facility, avoiding a costly arms race that would produce duplicate and unnecessary high-tech services. Leonard Pool, a short tempered and driven entrepreneur who had amassed a fortune through his creation of the Air Products Corporation, served as a board member of the Allentown Hospital. He pushed hard for the merger, anonymously donating

$5 million to the fundraising drive for the new facility. While the plan to fully merge the two facilities ran into stiff resistance, the building, designed with two separate towers, one for Sacred Heart and one for Allentown, combined with shared services was dedicated in 1974. In the end, Sacred Heart pulled out of this joint venture, choosing to remain at its original site. In 1975, Leonard Pool died, leaving $40 million dollars in a charitable trust whose purpose was to assure the success of the new hospital in meeting the healthcare needs of the region. Renamed Lehigh Valley Hospital after the pull out of Sacred Heart, the new hospital had a substantial endowment to assist in its development.

A decade later, Lehigh Valley Hospital tried to reinvent itself again to respond to changes in the reimbursement environment. The implementation of prospective payment by the Medicare program in 1984, shadowed by similar changes in payment by most of the other major health insurance plans that hospitals depended on for revenue, radically changed the environment. Until that time, hospitals essentially got paid what it cost to provide services. Now they began to be paid a flat rate per admission, no matter how long the patient stayed or how much it actually cost. Not surprisingly, both the length of stay and occupancy levels in hospitals dropped. The volume of admissions became critical to financial viability and competition for market share of profitable services heated up. A wave of corporate restructuring took place as hospitals tried to expand their inpatient market share and find alternative sources of revenue (Fleishman and Wlazelek, 1987). Swept along with this wave, Lehigh Valley Hospital renamed itself HealthEast and began an aggressive effort to expand and acquire new businesses. By 1990, it included more than 1,000 acute hospital beds, more than 5,000 employees and dominated health care delivery in the region. As government and private insurance payments increased the incentives to reduce the use and cost of acute inpatient care, the market became increasingly competitive. HealthEast took on the look and feel of a corporate conglomerate. It became a charter member of the Voluntary Hospitals of America (VHA), an organization that helped support this organizational transformation of its members. However, from the perspective of long time Allentown residents, even its new name reflected a grating arrogance and ambition that seemed out of place. As summarized in the much simplified diagram below (Fig. 2.1), HealthEast the parent company oversaw a charitable trust fund, more than

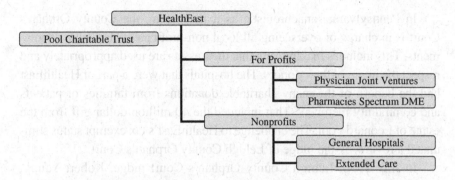

Fig. 2.1. HealthEast Simplified Organization Chart.

eight separate non-profit entities (hospitals, nursing homes, home health, hospice, etc.) and a shifting array of for-profit ventures. These for-profit arms of the company included Spectrum Medical Products, Inc. (a durable medical equipment company), a joint venture (50–50 partnership) with a group of physicians in a free standing surgical center, Spectrum Pharmacies, a healthcare information technology company and others. The idea was that the "profits" from these for-profit ventures would help subsidize the non-profit components. A few produced small profits, but others lost money. Local independent vendors complained of unfair competition. Decisions were made centrally by the top executives and HealthEast's board. The boards of the hospitals and other entities were relegated to a largely symbolic advisory role. Many community leaders were unhappy about these changes, but reluctant to voice their criticisms publicly for fear of a retaliation from this growing monolith.

Community Confrontation

In 1988, facing an economic downturn and struggling to balance their budgets, local school districts and municipalities challenged the tax exemption status of HealthEast and other non-profit hospitals in the region. The healthcare systems reacted with shock and disbelief that the local taxing bodies had the audacity to question them. "It was almost like it was unpatriotic to question whether hospitals should be a tax-exempt," one participant in these efforts observed (Garlicki, 1990).

In Pennsylvania, anachronistic as it may seem, the County Orphan's Court is in charge of overseeing all local non-profits and charitable endowments. This includes making sure that their assets are used appropriately and respect the intent of their donors. The hospitals that were a part of HealthEast had the benefit of the many charitable donations from families of patients and community members. That included the 40 million dollar gift from the estate of Leonard Pool. The challenge to HealthEast's tax exempt status stimulated a review by the judge of Lehigh County Orphan's Court.

In July 1990, Lehigh County Orphan's Court judge, Robert Young, after conducting interviews and a thorough audit of HealthEast, issued the following opinion:

> *If the trustees continue on the present course the hospitals will face expensive yearly tax challenges; discourage volunteerisms; incur the ire of the entire business community, lose control of the operation of their facilities to the medical profession; and no longer feel the justified pride they now deserve as trustees...If it ever becomes apparent that any non-profit organization is not properly carrying out its charitable purposes within Lehigh County, the court must remove those responsible and place such an entity in the hands of those persons who will fulfill its intended mission (Young, 1990).*

He urged the restructuring of HealthEast: (1) dissolving it as a holding company, (2) ending its for-profit ventures and (3) terminating the joint ambulatory surgery center venture with a group of physicians. Judge Young concluded that HealthEast was on a "collision course" with the people it served. An editorial in Allentown's *Morning Call* praised Judge Young's recommendations, observing that the "covenant with the community was being threatened by greed, expansionism and a subversion of the hospital's original mission of charity. It is a world of powerful, intimidating people. Judge Young himself was surprised by how much fear he encountered even among 'important citizens' who were afraid to discuss the business of the hospitals and physicians. This atmosphere of darkness may be suited to junk bond trading on the edge of the law, but not to a charitable hospital" (Morning Call, 1990).

Discussion

- Was the Morning Call's editorial a fair critique of the efforts of the executives of this recently merged health system?
- How could those involved in the governance of these hospitals have prevented the accusation of failing to attend to their charitable mission?

Postscript

The confrontation in the orphan's court sent shock waves through HealthEast, Pennsylvania and the rest of the nation. Its top managers were dismissed, the HealthEast name was abandoned and some restructuring took place to provide greater local board control. A major effort to look at community needs and explore ways to address them was undertaken. Other facilities in Pennsylvania and around the country followed suit, doing community needs assessments to get a better handle on their role in providing community benefit.

Like everything else in healthcare, the efforts to assure that these voluntary organizations lived up to their purpose were cumbersome, had plenty of loopholes and were not particularly effective in changing behavior or quieting the skeptics. In a period of increasing price competition brought about by the growth of managed care, hospital boards were not going to go out of their way to do things that they would lose money on. Indeed, most were concerned with generating profits or surpluses to create a larger "war chest" to update their physical plant and equipment, address growing competition and insulate themselves as best they could from anticipated future cuts in reimbursement.

Almost twenty years later in 2006, these efforts to assure the long term financial viability of Lehigh Valley Hospital again produced a scathing critique by Judge Young, now retired, in the form of a widely circulated "Unsolicited Opinion." "I think that most Americans believe that the health of our citizens (along with our security) is one of the prime responsibilities of government. We have not nationalized our hospitals; we have afforded them preferred tax status as long as they operate nonprofit facilities" (Young, 2006). In 2005, the hospital had accumulated a surplus of $76 million. The surplus that had precipitated the inquiry by

Young twenty years earlier was $17 million. Young called the 2005 surplus "both uncharitable and unacceptable" (Young, 2006). He noted that the earlier review was premised on the belief that, "whether caused by a desire for power or prestige, greed spoils charity which requires giving, not hording...there are plenty of unmet health needs in our county, yet it is apparent to me that the hospital leadership, rather than address them, continues its pursuit to create the premiere health provider on the Eastern Seaboard. Whether or not such a facility will be needed here in the future should be a community decision" (Young, 2006). Young demanded that the hospital board hold open meetings, make its full financial information public and hold a community wide conference to discuss their role as a charitable community hospital and how to lower healthcare costs. He suggested that if LVH failed to reform itself, then public officials should move to revoke its tax-exempt status and reinstate the Certificate of Need program.[1]

In the fiscal year 2007, Lehigh Valley Hospital and Health Network produced a $91 million dollar surplus, but was careful to label it on its website as "net available for community needs and debt repayment." It also gave a detailed accounting of the benefit its surplus provided the community in terms of making up for shortfalls in Medicare and Medicaid payment, bad debt, free care and educational and preventive services to the community, which they estimated at more than $127 million (Lehigh Valley Health Network, 2008). (Critics might argue that these benefits combined with the surplus really just amounted to cost shifting and higher prices passed on to the privately insured.) The website also provided a detailed background and bios on all its board members, an explanation of its policies used for determining compensation of its executives and a copy of its Internal Revenue Service 990 form. 990s are a detailed form all tax exempt charitable organizations are required to submit each year to the Internal Revenue Service describing compensation received by its board members, top executives and largest external vendors. The 990 also provides a detailed accounting in dollars of its community benefit. According to this document, the Chief Executive of LVH in Fiscal Year 2007 received

---

[1] See Chapter 6, Case 11: The Gift of the Heart, for an explanation of Certificate of Need.

a total compensation, benefits and expense package of $1.5 million and the total net assets or fund balance at the end of year had grown to $619 million (Lehigh Valley Health Network, 2008).

Sacred Heart, symbol of Leonard Pool's failure to rationalize hospital care in Allentown and avoid costly duplication of high-tech services, continues to operate independently, touting itself on its website as "big enough for the latest technology... small enough to make every patient matter" (Sacred Heart Hospital, 2009). It is equipped to do digital angiography, digital spot mammography, CT scans, MRIs and DEXA Scan tests for osteoporosis. Sacred Heart now also offers the still somewhat controversial bariatric surgery for the morbidly obese.

Both of these voluntary hospitals have done well in adapting to a changing environment and their patients have certainly benefited. Yet, the arms race continues, as does the growth in overall healthcare costs paid for by the citizens of Allentown. Even today in Allentown, some lack access to care other than through emergency rooms.

Discussion

- Who really are the owners of these hospitals and how do they exercise effective control?
- Part of the argument for locally owned non-profit hospitals is that they are more responsive to the communities they serve. Do the activities of the hospitals in Allentown support this argument? Explain.

Case 2: The AHERF Bankruptcy: Failure of Board Oversight[2]

Background

Allegheny Health, Education and Research Foundation (AHERF) in the 1990s didn't seem to be operating as a charitable organization but it

---

[2] The case relies heavily on information provided in two excellent accounts: Burns, L. R., J. Cacciamani *et al.* (2000). "The Fall of the House of AHERF: The Allegheny Bankruptcy." *Health Affairs* **19**: 7–41 and Massey, S. (1999). "Anatomy of a Bankruptcy." Retrieved September 15, 2008, 2008, from http://www.post-gazette.com/aherf/.

Fig. 2.2.   AHERF's Sherif Abdelhak (*Source*: Pittsburgh Post-Gazette (Massey, 1999)).

didn't seem to be operating as a business either. It mystified physicians and hospital administrators in Philadelphia, and was a constant source of gossip as they tried to figure out how to respond to the growing presence of this outsider in their medically conservative community. Philadelphia had six medical schools at the time and some estimate that until recently as many as 20% of physicians received at least some of their training in the Philadelphia area. Most of the American pharmaceutical industry originated in this region and Philadelphia's long and distinguished history of medical research and education had earned it the title "City of Medicine."

The competitive rivalry between Philadelphia and Pittsburgh ran much deeper than that of its professional football and baseball teams. The Philadelphia medical and business community had always considered themselves a cut above what existed in the urban metropolitan area at the western end of the state. Yet, Pittsburgh banks were buying up Philadelphia banks and Allegheny Hospital was using the cash from their highly profitable Pittsburgh operation to acquire hospitals and practices in the eastern end of the state.

Free standing hospitals and physicians in the Philadelphia metropolitan area market were approached with the same message. Any conversation with Philadelphia area primary care doctors, no matter what the purpose, soon reverted to "should I sell now or hold out?" AHERF was buying up primary care physician practices and offering large sums of money. If physicians waited, the price might go up even higher. Waiting might also make it impossible to earn a living or to sell their practice. The wave of restructuring taking place at that time was based on the vision of creating integrated delivery systems that included doctors, hospitals and other services so large and with such a dominant market share that health insurers could not risk not negotiating an acceptable contract with them.

As these systems evolved, they had begun to experiment with assuming risk, eliminating the "middle man" or insurance company and selling insurance products or packages of benefits directly to individuals and employers. It was a plausible idea and many believed that fully risk bearing capitated contracts between purchaser (employers or the government) and integrated delivery systems was the wave of the future.

Voluntary health insurance in the United States had originated from local "producers' cooperatives" like this, organized by local hospitals and medical societies. Beginning in the 1930s, these efforts had created the system of Blue Cross and Blue Shield plans. In Philadelphia and other markets the Blue Cross plans had begun in the 1970's to have an increasingly strained relationship with hospitals and physicians. They had adopted an adversarial role, dividing and conquering by selectively negotiating contracts with providers, playing off one against the other. If Blue Cross or the integrated delivery systems "won" and achieved total market dominance, nobody wanted to be on the outside looking in. In essence, AHERF was flying the same banner Benjamin Franklin had created during the French and Indian War in colonial times, telling the hospitals and physicians to "Join, or Die" (Fig. 2.3). It was with this aggressive approach that AHERF entered the Philadelphia market.

The Origins of AHERF and the AHERF Vision

In 1983, AHERF was established as a non-profit corporation. The sole member of this corporation was Allegheny General Hospital (AGH). A 670 bed hospital with a modest teaching affiliation with the University of Pittsburgh

Fig. 2.3.   AHERF's Recruitment Strategy.

Medical Center, Alleghany had long been the most profitable general hospital in the state. Yet, it was increasingly overshadowed by the University of Pittsburgh Medical Center's (UPMC) growing reputation as a national and international referral center. This irked Allegheny General's board chairman William Penn Snyder and the hospital's medical staff. Efforts to create a partnership with the UPMC that would assure a continued flow of tertiary care cases to AGH, a key source of their profitability, fell apart. UPMC felt threatened by AGH's market dominance in the region, growing endowment and loyal medical staff. Seeking to build on its medical school franchise, UPMC sought to undercut AGH by pulling some residency programs out of AGH. It was clear that Pittsburgh was not big enough for the ambitions of both of these entities. Snyder and the AGH board began a search for a new CEO that would lead the quest to acquire a medical school, secure its residency programs and transform AGH into a premier medical education and research institution. In 1986, they hired AGH's former Chief Operating Officer, Sherif Abdelhak, to spearhead this effort.

For Abdelhak and AGH's board, a struggling Philadelphia medical school was ripe for plucking. The idea of creating a statewide integrated delivery system seemed almost an afterthought, a way of rationalizing the acquisition. However, it soon took on a life of its own. The overall strategy as it evolved became: (1) creating a statewide integrated delivery system centered around an academic medicine core, (2) acquiring market share through the acquisition of primary care practices to leverage managed care contracts, (3) acquiring full risk capitated managed care contracts, (4) using the acquisition of smaller suburban hospitals to help fill urban teaching hospital beds and (5) using all of these assets to create synergies and economies of scale.

AHERF's Rapid Growth

Abdelhak, with the support of the AHERF board, went on a buying spree. In 1987, they acquired The Medical College of Pennsylvania, along with its two affiliated hospitals in Philadelphia, MCP Hospital and Eastern Pennsylvania Psychiatric Institute. Years before, MCP's name had been Women's Medical College of Pennsylvania. It was one of the few places where women could enroll and get a medical degree prior to the 1960s, but times had changed; it was struggling and needed an infusion of capital. In 1991, Abdelhak acquired United Hospitals, Inc. United Hospitals, Inc. began as St. Christopher's, a children's hospital in North Philadelphia, an impoverished minority neighborhood. It had acquired three struggling small suburban hospitals and renamed itself United Hospitals. The hope was that the suburban hospitals would help support the mission of the children's hospital, but it never panned out. In 1993, Abdelhak acquired Hahnemann Medical College and its affiliated hospital, merging the two medical schools into MCP-Hahnemann. This merger was followed up by aggressive recruitment of clinicians and researchers to enhance AHERF's research funding and stature, the acquisition of the six hospitals of the Graduate Health System in Philadelphia and the establishment of a western division in 1997 to operate its new community hospital affiliates in the Pittsburgh area (Forbes, Allegheny Valley and Canonsburg).

As illustrated in Fig. 2.4, in just ten years AHERF had been transformed from a single community hospital into a vast statewide empire that included fifteen hospitals, 29,590 employees, and a physician practice plan with more than 500 physicians. Moreover, its Philadelphia based Allegheny University of the Health Sciences was enrolling 3,300 students a year. AHERF and its affiliates reported total revenues of $2.05 billion in the 1997 fiscal year. Nothing, it seemed, could stop this juggernaut.

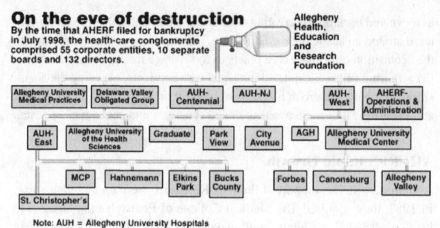

Fig. 2.4.   AHERF Organization Chart 1998 (*Source*: Pittsburgh Post-Gazette (Massey, 1999)).

Failure of Board Oversight

Beneath the surface, however, AHERF was accelerating towards a crash while most of its board members had been transformed from navigators guiding its course into passive passengers. The underlying assumptions of the strategic plan and forecast results were never critically debated or reviewed. Left partly concealed and unattended to were the financing mechanisms used to fuel the growth; these included internal subsidies, hidden internal cash transfers, raids on hospital endowments and the staggering accumulation of debt. While it came close to breaking even on its acute care, it continued to incur huge losses on the physician practices it had acquired. In addition, many of its assumptions concerning its risk-based insurance contracts and anticipated revenues from Medicaid and Medicare proved overly optimistic and those shortfalls added to the deficit. In just ten years, AHERF went from what was widely regarded as the "Fort Knox of hospitals" with a 15% profit margin ($36 million), only $67 million in debt and one of only forty in the nation with a top "Aa" bond rating, to an entity that was losing $330 million a year and had accumulated debts of $1.3 billion. How could this have happened?

AHERF had a parent board ranging between 25 and 35 members, more than twice the size that is generally recommended for effective governance. Compounding the problem, AHERF encompassed ten subsidiary boards responsible for the operations of its fifty-five corporate entities. There was no clearly interpretable information provided to subsidiary board members about what was happening elsewhere in AHERF's far flung empire. In an effectively functioning governance structure, such information would have been supplied. There were also some apparent conflicts of interest on the parent board. Five board members were current or former top executives of the Mellon Bank. A loan of $89 million was repaid to a bank consortium, including Mellon, without board discussion or approval, just three months before AHERF filed for bankruptcy protection.

The biggest problem, most observers agreed, was Abdelhak's domination of board decisions and his strong alliance with AHERF board chairman William Penn Snyder III. It was an odd couple.

Snyder, a descendent of one of Pennsylvania's first governors and named after the founder of Pennsylvania whose statue stands atop City Hall in Philadelphia, had been on the Board of Allegheny General since 1965. Snyder family members had served on the Board for almost all the time since its founding in 1885. His grandfather, William Penn Snyder, had founded the Shenango Furnace Company in 1906, playing a key role in the development of the steel industry in Pittsburgh. A handsome, tall, energetic and charming man, William Penn Snyder III or "Bill" as he was called, had helped lead the revitalization of Pittsburgh and was considered one of its social pillars.

In contrast, Sherif Abdelhak was born and raised in Egypt in a family at odds with the ruling elite. He got a BA degree in economics from the American University in Cairo in 1968. Immigrating to the United States, he began his healthcare career in the purchasing department of Allegheny General Hospital. He was the "fixer" from whom medical staff members could quickly get the equipment they needed and he earned their favor in this way. He climbed in the subsequent eleven years to Chief Operating Officer. During this period he received an MBA degree going to school part-time at the Katz Graduate School of Business at the University of Pittsburgh. In 1982, he left AGH to become CEO of a local health system only to be recruited back in 1986 by Snyder as the new CEO. Snyder had become increasingly frustrated by the slow, methodical, consensus building approach of AGH's former CEO, who had impeccable credentials and a national reputation. He was impressed by Abdelhak's aggressive and decisive approach to solving problems and his medical staff support. Snyder saw an attack dog that could address the threat of UPMC and realize his ambitions for AGH. They became partners in pushing this agenda forward and overcoming board and other resistance.

It was a formidable partnership. Board meetings were described as scripted affairs intentionally staged to limit oversight and participation by board members. For example, board members might receive as much as one thousand pages in a binder for review shortly before a brief board meeting. "Half of the people didn't even open the book. They didn't have the time," one board member observed (Massey, 1999). As a result, they relied on Abdelhak and Snyder's judgment and in turn, the elderly Snyder may have relied on Abdelhak, who made him feel involved in the management of the enterprise. Thus, in many cases, key decisions were made without providing prior review by the board and, in some cases, the board was not informed of these decisions at all. In negotiating with Vanguard for the purchase of the Philadelphia area hospitals during AHERF's final death spiral, the CEO of Vanguard was surprised when Abdelhak told him, "When you're talking to me, you're talking to the board. I have the authority to make this happen" (Massey, 1999).

It would be, however, too easy and too comforting to blame Abdelhak solely for the demise of AHERF. Too many people with responsibilities to AHERF just went along for the ride because it did not pay them personally to make waves.

Non-profit hospital boards typically are less prone to making risky investments than those of for-profit corporations. They view their major role as fiduciary, and see their job as being responsible for protecting assets and endowment and not investing it all on a high stakes gamble. Historically, board members included many major donors who were conservative custodians of "their" money. As a result, voluntary hospitals are typically much less highly leveraged or risk prone than those of for-profit hospital systems. Yet, perhaps lulled into complacency by a long history of financial strength and overwhelmed by the pace and complexity of AHERF's growth, they failed to challenge the decisions made by Abdelhak's management team.

Top AHERF managers who may have had misgivings about the reckless pace of acquisitions and growing financial vulnerability did not voice their objections either. Not being a team player meant either resigning or being fired. Most were receiving salary and bonuses well above market rates and were becoming accustomed to a lifestyle they could not have envisioned a few years earlier. (More than 77 managers were making at least $200,000 and Abdelhak's salary and benefit package exceeded $1 million, as did that of more than a half a dozen doctors.)

Outside experts hired to help guide AHERF were also silent. The management and human resource consulting firm that helped the board set their executive compensation rates viewed the growing AHERF empire as a key revenue stream for their business and were not about to disappoint Abdelhak and the rest of his management team with more conservative compensation recommendations. More critically, outside auditors who are supposed to provide the key information about the financial health of operations to assist in board decisions, failed to do so. AHERF used Coopers and Lybrand, who had served as the auditor for AGH since its inception and it gave AHERF a clean bill of health in its last audit in June, 1997. Hired by management, Coopers and Lybrand had every incentive to portray the results in a positive light. Coopers was later replaced, but only after the AHERF bankruptcy. Long before, there had been warning signs. For example, the Coopers and Lybrand Pittsburgh office was found guilty by a federal jury of negligence in a regional drug store chain's fraud and embezzlement scheme in 1996.

Another source of information important in board decisions are the bond rating agencies. Since non-profit health systems relied heavily on tax exempt bonds to finance their long term debt, bond ratings which define the risk to investors, determine the cost of such borrowing, or even whether it is possible at all. Health firms pay bond rating agencies to produce these reports which, not surprisingly can tend to be more generous to their customer. The health firm can also purchase bond insurance to improve the bond rating, reducing risk for the prospective bond holder, but masking the underlying financial status of The health system issuing the bonds. The bond insuring firms can all "re-insure" the risk they have assumed, redistributing much of it to others. Up until the AHERF bank-ruptcy, the risks of default, particularly for large health systems were per-ceived as minimal or non-existent. Hospitals got the majority of their revenue from public sources and it seemed politically unthinkable that publicly elected officials would allow a large hospital system to fail. The ultimate consequence of all of these layers of insulation surrounding the true financial status of AHERF was that absolutely no one was minding the store. Indeed, in many respects, AHERF's failures were a microcosm and a forewarning of the failures that would produce global financial collapse in 2008.

The AHERF Bankruptcy

In the spring of 1998, losses to the AHERF system were approaching $1 million dollars a day. Bill Snyder had been deluged with complaints that AHERF was not paying its bills. The reserves were running dry in spite of all the efforts to cut costs by laying off more than 1,200 employees and the closing of one hospital. Both Medicare and the state Medicaid program cuts were reducing anticipated inpatient revenue and AHERF was also incurring substantial losses from risk sharing contracts with both the local Blue Cross plan and the largest commercial plan. The only option seemed to be to find a buyer for most of the Philadelphia area operations and at least save AGH, the Pittsburgh mother ship. Meeting with his top managers in April, Abdelhak demanded more budget cuts. This was on top of previ-ous cuts and layoffs. Donald Kay, head of the AHERF Philadelphia area operations, protested that he had to perform mandatory repairs of a hospi-tal sprinkler system or he would go to jail. "Then go to jail, I've done everything for you," Abdelhak exploded (Massey, 1999). Nurses were beginning to complain about a shortage of supplies as vendors began to put AHERF facilities on a cash only basis. A consortium of banks, including Mellon concluded that AHERF was not generating enough cash to remain in compliance with its $100 million line of credit and demanded repay-ment. Without getting the board approval as required, Abdelhak transferred funds from an endowment account to provide the $86 million the bank consortium was demanding. On Sunday of Memorial Day weekend, Snyder called, met with Abdelhak and fired him. In June, Vanguard, the only remaining national for profit chain interested in acquiring the AHERF Philadelphia operation got cold feet and withdrew their offer. AHERF was out of options and on July 21, it filed for Chapter 11 bankruptcy.

Discussion

- Why did AHERF's strategic plan, as guided by Sherif Abdelhak and William Penn Snyder fail?
- What changes in the board and the way the governance process operated in AHERF might have prevented its financial collapse?

Postscript

The AHERF bankruptcy story, of course, was repeated on a grander scale in the global financial market crisis ten years later in 2008. None of the conflicts of interest of bond rating agencies or concealment of risks through insurance had been corrected and the excesses of managers and the risks to which they exposed their owners make the behavior of the AHERF managers seem modest in comparison.

Indeed, the effort to punish the perpetrators of the AHERF crash, or at least some credible scapegoats, ended with little to show for the effort. 1,500 charges were brought against Abdelhak by the Pennsylvania Attorney General. Similar charges were initiated against AHERF's General Counsel Nancy Wynstra and Chief Financial Officer David McConnell. All charges against Wynstra were dismissed. McConnell was set for criminal trial on one charge but entered an accelerated rehabilitative disposition program for non-violent first-time offenders and did not stand trial. Abdelhek pleaded no contest to a single misdemeanor related to the inappropriate use of endowment funds. He was sentenced to 11–23 months in Allegheny County jail, but was paroled after three months (Cobb and Hotchkiss, 2004). The SEC settled fraud charges against McConnell with a $25,000 fine and barred him from practicing before the SEC for three years. Three AHERF auditors received similar sanctions. Abdelhak was the only person who served jail time. Many of his excesses (a private corporate jet, executive retreats in lavish international resorts, waiver of the admission requirements for his wife to

Allegheny medical school, etc) did not play well in the press or in court (Massey, 1999). Yet, there was no evidence he personally benefited from any of the illegally transferred funds that went into trying to keep AHERF afloat. Divorced, having gone through a personal bankruptcy filing and facing a U.S. Tax Court order to pay $500,000 in back taxes, he lives in exile in Kentucky. "I don't have a life. They managed to destroy it ten years ago" (Fitzpatrick, 2007). He still believes he could have saved AHERF if he had had just a little more time.

Dealing with the debts and assets of the bankrupt estate was a complex and protracted affair. At the time of the bankruptcy filing, creditors were owed $1.3 billion, including $605 million in bond debt, $447 million in unsecured debt and $200 million in loans to the eastern AHERF operations. Much of the approximate $206 million in charitable assets in the form of endowments and other restricted funds, which had accumulated over many years through gifts and tax exemptions, had apparently been raided. The eastern facilities were finally sold to Tenet, a for-profit hospital chain for $345 million. From the proceeds of the Tenet sale, $200 million was set aside to keep the hospitals open and fund operations, $50 million was allocated to the endowment of Drexel University in return for taking over the management of the medical school (increasing their endowment by 33%) and $40 million was awarded to Tenet to handle the anticipated malpractice insurance payments. There were also additional expenses in managing the bankruptcy transactions. Mellon Bank returned $28 million to the estate to settle claims that senior executives had used their positions on the AHERF board to get preferential treatment in collecting debts owed by AHERF and various insurers paid the AHERF estate approximately $60 million. The efforts of the committee of unsecured creditors to sue Coopers and Lybrand, AHERF's auditor (now Price, Waterhouse and Coopers), for damages failed in Federal District court in 2007. Unsecured creditors ended up receiving 17 cents on the dollar and, after a decade, the costly bankruptcy proceedings have largely come to an end (Cobb and Hotchkiss, 2004).

The human and social costs of this bankruptcy were incalculable. All of its 30,000 employees faced the stress and uncertainty and many lost their jobs, faced difficult transitions and have yet to fully recover. Tenet has since closed three of the eight community hospitals for which it assumed responsibility, each with long ties to their local communities. Their demise, particularly in the case of the Medical College of Pennsylvania Hospital, was a difficult and drawn out struggle in a community deeply troubled by the loss. More generally, the AHERF bankruptcy had a chilling effect on the ability of non-profit voluntary hospitals, particularly the remaining independent ones in less affluent communities, to get the financing necessary for the renovation and replacement of aging physical plants. Half a dozen facilities in the Philadelphia area have closed. In a state where no for-profit hospitals previously existed, 22 have been acquired by national for-profit chains, providing a source of capital, but also severing ties with communities that previously had helped guide and plan the long term future of their hospitals. No health system today, for-profit or non-profit, talks about a grand vision of a seamless integrated system of care supported by risk assuming capitated contracts. Health providers are focused more on targeting profitable specialty niches, leaving communities and families pretty much to fend for themselves in an increasingly fragmented healthcare market. The cost and casualties of these developments, at least in part, could be included in those of the AHERF bankruptcy.

The assumptions underlying AHERF's behavior, however, illustrate more profound problems in the rational organization of healthcare in the United States. While more reckless, there was nothing original in the strategy adopted by AHERF. Part of Abdelhak's success in getting board members and others to embrace his vision and strategy, was that it was an attractive and logical one. Most other academic health centers in Pennsylvania (e.g. University of Pittsburgh, University of Pennsylvania and the Jefferson University Health Systems) pursued similar strategies of expansion, as did academic health systems in other areas of the country. Indeed, in most other developed countries, the government has played a similar role pursuing a similar vision in shaping and organizing their health systems. The University of Pittsburgh and the University of Pennsylvania Health Systems faced many of the same difficulties that AHERF faced in implementing this vision, as did academic health centers elsewhere. They have regrouped, adapted to the existing market and reimbursement environment, and most are doing well. Other developed countries have persisted in the evolution of this vision and, at least in terms of cost and quality comparisons to the United States, described in Chapter 1, have done reasonably well.

There were two key problems that AHERF and other academic health systems in the United States faced in implementing this strategy that nationalized health systems did not.

First, the need for the tertiary care services provided by an academic health center is a rare event. It would be almost impossible to buy enough primary care practices and general community hospitals to "feed" enough referrals to a tertiary care hospital in a self-contained integrated delivery system. The population that such a network would have to be responsible for would be in the millions.

Secondly, even if it were possible to acquire a large enough network to generate the necessary volume of tertiary care referrals, it would probably be illegal. A network of that size would involve such a large market share in a region; it would be a monopoly and run afoul of anti-trust law. In addition, even if a network of this size was achieved, it would be difficult legally to capture all of these referrals. Doctors in the practices "owned" by the health system could not be required to refer their patients nor be provided financial incentives to do so. This is called physician self-referral and the "Stark" regulations (a federal law passed in 1993), with a few exceptions, prohibits it. It is the most recent effort to curb the abuses of "fee splitting" that professional reforms a century ago attempted to address. Fee splitting was the practice of referring physicians negotiating a percentage of the fee charged by a surgeon as a "kickback" and clearly violated the trust of a patient and the ethics of their referring physician.

Some might argue that "you can't get there from here" and that this vision can only be realized in a publicly owned or a public utility model of a National Health Service or single payer universal health system. A market based health system whose public regulations are focused on preventing anti-competitive behavior and protecting the consumer from the self–serving collusion of service providers certainly presents barriers to such efforts.

Discussion

- How might such a vision be realized in the absence of public ownership or is such a goal an illusion?

3

The Medical Staff: Villains or Victims?

Organizing the Medical Staff[3]

Understanding how a medical staff works is the key to understanding how hospitals and most other health-related organizations work. In most cases in the United States, the medical staff is a voluntary body composed mostly of independent practitioners. They serve as the gatekeepers, determining who will be permitted to admit patients and what a physician will be permitted to do with those admitted. They oversee the quality of care of their members in an institution that serves as their cooperative workshop. It is a voluntary, self- policing body. Given the pressures on members involved in running their own practices, the inevitable financial conflicts of interest among their practices, those of other medical staff members and those of the hospital itself, it is remarkable that it works at all. Physicians denied privileges or disciplined by a medical staff suffer economic harm and can sue. In decisions involving grey areas, there may often be a strong temptation to avoid the additional aggravation and time involved in refusing privileges or disciplining a colleague. Medical staff members may prefer to look the other way, rather than bring a complaint that may embroil them in a lengthy and difficult review process. In addition, hospitals, financially dependent on admissions from physicians, are reluctant to press the medical staff for rigorous policing of its members. Yet, it generally works reasonably well.

---

[3] This history of medical staff development summarizes material published elsewhere: Smith, D. B. (2001). *Long Term Care in Transition: The Regulation of Nursing Homes.* Washington, D.C., Beard Books. pp. 1–6.

The organized medical staff was a part of the creation of the modern hospital. It was a key element of the hospital standardization reform movement of the American College of Surgeons. In 1900, the only real controls over healthcare were the individual consciences of providers and the willingness of the general public to pay for their services or products. Medicine was fragmented into rival factions with conflicting doctrines. State licensing laws were largely ineffective in ensuring a minimal level of competence. A hospital could be any building one wished to label as such. There were no standards. Proprietary schools dominated the training of physicians. Most medical schools were open to high school graduates and many waived even this requirement. Many of the proprietary schools were operated as profit-making businesses. Instruction within them often consisted of nothing more than a series of large lectures, and students graduated without ever hearing a heartbeat or feeling the pulse of a patient. The more marginal schools were diploma mills.

Abuses within the profession itself were rampant. Fee-splitting or kickbacks for surgical referrals were common practice. Fortunes were made with quack cures.

As the scientific basis of medicine grew, the influence of its practitioners grew as well. In general, professional controls become feasible only when those pressing for them can make a persuasive argument for their social usefulness. That point was apparently reached about 1912 when, as one medical scientist observed, "it became possible to say of the United States that a random patient with a random disease consulting a doctor at random stood a better than fifty-fifty chance of benefiting from the encounter"(Somers and Somers, 1961).

A methodical house cleaning began. Entry into the medical profession was restricted, training standards raised, hospital conditions improved, and attempts to police the ethics of medical practice increased. The emergence of medical staff control over hospitals was a byproduct of the reform efforts of the American College of Surgeons. Established in 1913 as an independent professional association, the College faced the immediate problem of determining who was eligible for membership. An evaluation of the surgeon's work was essential. However, hospitals did not keep adequate records to make such assessments possible and there was little or no effort by the hospital's own medical staff to evaluate such performance.

The College shifted part of its focus to addressing this problem. They began a program to survey and certify hospitals. The initial standards for approval were drawn up by a committee chaired by Ernest Codman and included what Codman described as "end result analysis," to determine whether the treatment was as effective as possible (Christoffel, 1976). In the first survey, in 1918, the College found that of 6,921 hospitals with more than 100 beds, only 89 met their minimum standards. The findings were appalling since many of the leading medical centers failed the test. Concerned about the consequences of releasing the names of these institutions, all copies of the report were burned in the basement furnace of the hotel in New York where the committee met to deliberate. The revised standard placed more emphasis on structure; a record keeping system, a set of standard procedures and documentation. Only recently has interest in documenting end results or outcomes resurfaced. In 1920, the College published the first list of hospitals in the United States that met their revised standards. Those standards focused and largely continue to focus on five basic areas.

1. **Organization:** Physicians and surgeons privileged to practice in a hospital must be organized into a group to oversee and take responsibility for the medical care provided in the hospital.
2. **Membership:** Membership in the medical staff shall be restricted to physicians and surgeons who are (a) competent in their respective fields and (b) "worthy in character and in matters of professional ethics."
3. **Management:** The staff, with the approval of the governing board, shall adopt rules and policies governing medical practice, including regular meetings and review of the clinical experience of various departments and individual medical staff members.
4. **Records:** Accurate and complete standardized case records for all patients.
5. **Facilities:** Adequate laboratory and diagnostic facilities for the medical diagnosis and treatment of patients should be available and overseen by trained technicians.

The American College of Surgeons hospital standardization initiative was, of course, a voluntary self-improvement process and proceeded accordingly. Having no legal sanctions, it relied on persuasion and the good will of the institutions. The hospital "visitors" as they were called (not inspectors) were carefully instructed:

> The visitor is to collect facts and he is to collect facts only with the good will and approval of the respective hospitals. His mission is business. He is not a detective, an unbidden critic nor a social caller. *He is not to make comparisons of one institution with another.* He is to be helpful and constructive. The success of his visit will depend much upon his sincerity. He must believe in his work. The visitor who is unwelcome has in all probability not wisely handled the situation."(American College of Surgeons, 1920, p. 544 italics added)

Hospitals were notified several months in advance of visits. The College reported widespread cooperation with the program. As one physician is reported to have said, "It is wise that we lead now in a program for better care of patients rather than be forced later by the public to follow such a program" (American College of Surgeons, 1920, p. 544). That argument has echoed in debates over professional control ever since.

The American College of Surgeons hospital standardization effort was remarkably successful. It established the basic pattern of quality control that continues with elaboration and refinement today. In 1952, the responsibility for the program was shifted to a newly established Joint Commission on the Accreditation of Hospitals, representing the American College of Surgeons, The American College of Physicians, The American Medical Association, the American Hospital Association and the Canadian Hospital Association.

The American College of Surgeons' effort succeeded in assigning almost exclusive responsibility for the quality of care provided by physicians in a hospital to its medical staff. Up until the 1950s, few states even had hospital licensure laws and even since then, state licensure bodies have remained in the shadows, understaffed and largely focused on life safety and construction codes. Only with the implementation of the Medicare-Medicaid legislation in 1965 did the public *laissez-faire* attitude toward quality oversight shift. Medicare regulations spelled out minimum standards for the receipt of Medicare funds, modeling their standards after those of the Joint Commission. Indeed, hospitals that were accredited by the Joint Commission had "deemed status" to receive Medicare funds. That is, accredited hospitals were assumed to meet the Medicare standards. While it gave the Joint Commission powerful new leverage over the nation's hospitals, it also drew them into an ideologically uneasy alliance with the federal government which continues to the present. Indeed, after the passage of Medicare, emissaries from the Social Security Administration met with and asked that the Joint Commission change its bylaws to include a federal government representative on their board. This suggestion was greeted with indignation and quickly abandoned. A public member was added several decades later. Growing pressures for greater public accountability have more recently led to the formation of an awkward alliance, the Hospital Quality Alliance, which includes the federal Medicare program and the Joint Commission. Comparative quality measures developed by the Joint Commission for all hospitals in the United States are now publicly available on Medicare's Hospital Compare web site.

The hospital standardization effort gave the hospital's medical staff the major responsibility for overseeing the quality of the medical care provided. However, as the two cases presented in this chapter illustrate, hospital medical staffs have the same imperfections as other voluntary organizations. The selection of members and the disciplining of them are shaped by political, social and economic concerns that often are at odds with the stated purpose. Case 3 involves a whistle-blower physician whose suspicious death was related to racial disparities in treatment that still persist today. Case 4 involves a medical staff that looked the other way, permitting questionable surgery to be performed that resulted in the revocation of the surgeon's license by the state medical licensure board and embroiled the hospital in a series of malpractice cases.

Case 3: The Mysterious Death of a Mobile Infirmary Medical Staff Member[4]

In the dark early morning hours of Sunday, January 27, 1967, in Mobile, Alabama, Dr. Jean Cowsert was apparently awakened by the sound of

---

[4] Based on research supported by Robert Wood Johns Health Policy Investigator Award, published in: Smith, D. B. (1999). *Health Care Divided: Race and Healing a Nation*. Ann Arbor, University of Michigan Press.

glass breaking in her kitchen window. She was found dead at 7:00 AM near her front steps, clad in pajamas and a bathrobe, fatally wounded in the chest by a single shot from a foreign made 38-caliber revolver (Mobile Register, 1967). The weapon, owned by Dr. Cowsert, was found underneath her body. Two days later, the death was ruled an accident. Surrounding her death and unknown to those investigating it, however, a bitter, protracted test of wills swirled between the Federal government, Mobile's largest hospital and its medical staff.

Up until 1965, medical and hospital care in Mobile had been divided strictly by race. The 540 bed Mobile Infirmary, the dominant institution in the region's social and medical hierarchy, served whites only. The 35-bed Saint Martin de Porres Hospital served the private paying blacks of Mobile and was the only facility where black dentists and physicians could obtain privileges. Two additional hospitals with antebellum roots served both races: Mobile General Hospital, a 247 bed county facility for the indigent and Providence Hospital, a 262 bed facility operated by the Daughters of Charity of St. Vincent de Paul. Care in these two facilities was strictly segregated by race. The hospitals of Mobile served a population of about 500,000, of which one third was black (Department of Health Education and Welfare, 1967). All four of these facilities had received substantial federal funds for their construction from the Hill-Burton program for which Senator Lister Hill (D, Alabama) was the major architect. While the Hill-Burton legislation prohibited racial discrimination, it specifically allowed, as no other Federal legislation in the 20th century, for the allocation of those funds on a "separate but equal" basis. Often such arrangements, as the organization of hospital services in Mobile clearly illustrated, were certainly separate but hardly equal.

Title VI of the 1964 Civil Rights Act prohibited use of federal funds on a "separate but equal" basis. The ultimate test of the Federal will to enforce this prohibition, however, lay not in the award of Hill-Burton funds, but in the control of the massive infusion of new Federal dollars that would begin with the implementation of the Medicare program on July 1, 1966.

The Office of Equal Health Opportunity (OEHO) in the Public Health Service, a hastily cobbled together operation that relied on ill-prepared temporary "volunteer" transfers from other parts of the Department of Health, Education and Welfare (DHEW) bureaucracy, was responsible for the Title VI certification of facilities that wished to participate in the Medicare program. The real key to the effectiveness of the effort, however, lay in an elaborate intelligence network of local civil rights groups, leaders in local chapters of the National Medical Association and black hospital employees. This network monitored, supplied intelligence of noncompliance and, in many cases, directed local federal enforcement efforts.

The combination of an aggressive army of volunteer Federal enforcement agents insulated from congressional pressures, a grass roots intelligence network and the lure of a massive flow of federal funds to hospitals had, on the surface, produced a remarkable transformation. The four hospitals in Mobile, however, were among the remaining 327 across the nation still awaiting Title VI clearance on June 30, 1966. Among the four Mobile hospitals, Providence had made the most significant progress toward integration of its accommodations. In August 1965, the local civil rights group withdrew its complaint against Providence Hospital, informing Federal officials that the facility had followed a determined policy to comply with Title VI (LaFlore, 1965). Yet, these steps proved painful ones for Providence, whose census dropped significantly as white patients shifted their admission to the Mobile Infirmary (Chapman, 1995). Perhaps reluctant to single out an individual hospital for certification and exacerbate the problem that Providence had already experienced, the OEHO had yet to certify any of the hospitals in Mobile. Providence, Mobile General and Saint Martin de Porres finally received Title VI certification for Medicare funding on July 1st. The Mobile Infirmary, the city's largest and best-equipped facility, did not.

The decision not to certify the Infirmary plunged OEHO for the first time into the murky waters of Title VI enforcement in medical practice. Medical practice, or at least its payment under Part B of the Medicare program, had been exempted from Title VI compliance. DHEW's legal counsel had developed a convoluted rationale for this, but the real reasons were practical and political. No one could figure out what Title VI compliance would mean in the private fee for service practice of medicine or how it could be monitored. Organized medicine, the local medical societies, state societies and the AMA were powerful political forces and reluctant, if not openly hostile participants in the Medicare program. Their cooperation was critical for the smooth implementation of the massive new program.

During the last six months of 1965, however, only ten of the 10,000 patients admitted to the Mobile Infirmary had been black (Department of Health Education and Welfare, 1967). The Infirmary claimed they had admitted every patient, regardless of race, referred by its medical staff and were in full compliance with Title VI. From the perspective of the staff of the OEHO, providing Title VI certification to the Infirmary whose physicians were selectively admitting on the basis of race would be tantamount to endorsing segregation. Similar racially selective hospital admission patterns existed in many communities, including northern ones such as Chicago (Young, 2007). OEHO hoped to use the Mobile Infirmary as a test case of the Title VI responsibilities of hospitals to assure that the admitting practices of their medical staffs were evenhanded. In interfering in this way with the practice of medicine, OEHO had touched a raw nerve and the battle lines were drawn.

Dr. Jean Cowsert had been drawn into these same murky waters and her involvement influenced OEHO's decision to use the Mobile Infirmary as a test case. An internist, she had graduated first in her 1954 class of the University of Alabama Medical School, one of two women in a class of 62 (Mobile Register, 1967). She had returned to her native Mobile in 1959 to practice. In 1966, she became President of the Providence Hospital medical staff and had been instrumental in guiding its integration effort. She also had medical staff privileges at the Mobile Infirmary and, as a participant in its staff meetings, subsequently served as a confidential informant to OEHO. In the vernacular of the cold war, and equally appropriate to the cold war waged over racial integration, she became a mole. She brought to the attention of OEHO an effort to use emergency admissions to circumvent Title VI requirements. She also provided a list of physicians on Mobile Infirmary's staff who were refusing to admit any of their black patients to the Infirmary, after the hospital had vehemently refused to provide OEHO with any information on the admission patterns of its individual medical staff members (LeFlore, 1966).

As the months without Medicare payments for the Mobile Infirmary dragged on, participants became more embittered and the pressure for some kind of settlement mounted. More than 100 beds and an entire wing lay empty at the Mobile Infirmary (Mobile Register, 1966). The Infirmary focused its significant political assets on DHEW. Pressure was brought to bear by Senator John Sparkman (D, AL), Senator Lister Hill (D, AL), Representative Jack Edwards (R, AL) and Mobile's Mayor Joseph Langan. to break the impasse. Even Governor George Wallace weighed in, describing the denial of a Medicare certification of the Infirmary as not only "heartless but the most immoral act I can imagine" and demanding a congressional investigation (Mobile Register, 1966).

In December, DHEW finally caved in to these pressures, agreeing to conduct a top-level review and taking control away from the embattled OEHO. Assistant Surgeon General, Leo Gehrig, was assigned to visit Mobile to broker a compromise. In preparation for the visit, OEHO staff briefed Dr. Gehrig. In addition to the admission statistics, Gehrig was provided with off-the-record information, including the identity of the Infirmary's medical staff informant, Dr. Cowsert. Meetings were held at the Infirmary with Dr. Gehrig in January and he returned to Washington believing that he had crafted a workable compromise. He told OEHO's staff that, in the process, he had the opportunity to confer with Dr. Cowsert on the phone from his hotel room. The OEHO staff was aghast, since those familiar with Federal civil rights investigations in the South at that time had to assume that such phone calls were being monitored. (In hotels at that time, all calls went through the hotel switchboard operator and so it was easy to listen in.)

Early on Monday morning on January 28, Robert Nash, the Director of OEHO in Washington, received a call from an administrator at the Mobile Infirmary informing him of Dr. Cowsert's death. The staff at OEHO concluded that there was no reason for such a call unless the administrator knew the relationship between OEHO and Dr. Cowsert and suspected foul play. Clearly, Dr. Cowsert's role as an informant had not remained a secret in Mobile.

Yet, DHEW caved. The Infirmary was soon notified of "interim" Title VI certification that would be retroactive to February 1, 1967 and Medicare funds began flowing to the hospital. OEHO staff had strongly opposed Gehrig's idea of interim certification since the Infirmary's board and medical staff had not budged. On June 28, 1967, the home of J. L. LeFlore, the leader of the local civil rights group that helped orchestrate the hospital integration efforts in Mobile was fire-bombed. The Infirmary received full Title VI certification for Medicare beginning in July 1967. In the last six months of 1967, the census of the Mobile Infirmary hit a record of 93%

and plans were completed for a six-story addition (Mobile Register, 1968). In the fall of 1967, Congress would finally force the elimination of OEHO and the consolidation of all civil rights activities into a single centralized DHEW Office for Civil Rights that would be easier to control. Many of the senior staff of OEHO either resigned or refused reassignment.

In April 1968, Martin Luther King was assassinated in Memphis. That event cast a shadow over all the other tumultuous and tragic events in that year. The death of Dr. Cowsert in Mobile, the high water mark of the only sustained Federal offensive to eliminate disparities in healthcare, disappeared from local memory and public records. No records now exist of the initial city police investigation of the death, the autopsy, the FBI investigation that was requested by OEHO staff, or in the archived correspondence of the local congressman that had assisted the Infirmary in gaining Medicare funds. In compliance with federal regulations, all the working files of OEHO staff related to the Mobile Infirmary case were destroyed long ago.

> *Oh, Mama, can this really be the end,*
> *To be stuck inside of Mobile*
> *With the Memphis blues again.*
> *(Dylan, 1966)*

Discussion

- Why did Dr. Cowsert break ranks with her medical staff colleagues and intervene, in spite of risk to both her livelihood as a physician and her life?
- Why did the staff of the Office of Equal Health Opportunity use the Mobile Infirmary as a test case, denying their certification for Medicare funds?

Postscript

Today the Mobile Infirmary, like other facilities in Mobile, is fully integrated. The Mobile Infirmary has roughly the same proportion of black patients as in the general population of the metropolitan area. Hospitals in

Mobile are now less segregated than they are in most northern cities. In addition, racial disparities in death rates are lower.

The peculiar adaptation of Mobile to the federal insistence on integration differs little from what has taken place in most metropolitan areas across the nation. All the hospitals in Mobile now have only single rooms, avoiding any concerns about race mixing, but no doubt adding significantly to the cost of care. Ironically, Providence Hospital, which courageously led the effort to integrate, has relocated to a more affluent and whiter section of Mobile. Mobile General, now the University of Southern Alabama Medical Center, perhaps best illustrates the peculiar nature of the accommodation and the absence of any institutional memory of it. Concerned over integrating seating in the lobby, the hospital removed the seats and converted the lobby into a "medical museum." Medical staff members were asked to contribute memorabilia, particularly from ancestors who served as surgeons in the Confederate Army during the Civil War. Up until 2000, patients and their families not only had no place to sit, but passed by display cases of saws and other instruments used to amputate limbs. While this no doubt caused some discomfort among the patients and their families, its symbolism initially provided some amusement among medical staff members who were resentful about the forced federal integration of their facility. No one apparently on its medical staff or working for the hospital now has any memory of why this collection is located in their lobby. However, concern about the rising value of this historical collection located unprotected in a public lobby motivated efforts to move it to a more secure area and one can only hope that the seating has returned.

The loss of the Mobile Infirmary test case still shapes the American healthcare system in peculiar ways. As a result, no federal effort was ever mounted to collect information about the referral and practice patterns of physicians by race. Research studies, however, continue to document substantial racial disparities in treatment and referral patterns that cannot be fully explained by insurance coverage.

Discussion

- What explains these persistent disparities and what should be done about them?

Case 4: South Park Hospital and the Limits of Medical Staff Oversight[5]

Background

South Park Hospital is a 50 bed general hospital located in a rural community in the south whose attractive vistas and climate have made it a growing retirement destination. Its 150 physicians and 650 employees serve a population in the area of about 60,000. The hospital is a member of a non-profit system that includes hospitals in ten states and almost 6,000 licensed beds. South Park staff, according to its CEO, "believe that a wholesome lifestyle contributes to good physical, mental and spiritual well being. Its medical staff and employees draw motivation from six strongly held principles: a Christian mission and values; excellence in the service we provide to our patients, our community and staff; compassion; focus on community wellness; high ethical standards; and cultural diversity. These principles guide the manner in which we treat each other and those we serve."

South Park Hospital has an active "Performance Improvement Committee" that reviews and seeks process improvement in surgical cases and other aspects of care at the hospital. It follows all the guidelines of the Joint Commission in terms of credentialing and re-credentialing prospective medical staff members. After correcting some minor deficiencies, the hospital received "Accreditation with Full Compliance," The Joint Commission's good housekeeping seal of approval at the end of 2003.

Chronic Pain

As many as 86 million people suffer to some degree from a vague assortment of debilitating symptoms labeled "chronic pain syndrome." Chronic pain syndrome is a condition for which medicine has yet to understand the causes and for which no agreed upon treatment exists. It affects the quality of life and economic security not only of the person with pain,

---

[5] Names and some of the details in this case have been altered to assure confidentiality.

but also his or her family. US business and industry lose about $90 million annually to sick time, reduced productivity, and direct medical and other benefit costs due to chronic pain among employees. The current state of knowledge about chronic pain syndrome as described on the National Institute of Health website is summarized below:

Chronic Pain Information Page

What is Chronic Pain?

While acute pain is a normal sensation triggered in the nervous system to alert you to possible injury and the need to take care of yourself, chronic pain is different. Chronic pain persists. Pain signals keep firing in the nervous system for weeks, months, even years. There may have been an initial mishap — sprained back, serious infection, or there may be an ongoing cause of pain — arthritis, cancer, ear infection, but some people suffer chronic pain in the absence of any past injury or evidence of body damage. Many chronic pain conditions affect older adults. Common chronic pain complaints include headache, low back pain, cancer pain, arthritis pain, Neutrogena pain (pain resulting from damage to the peripheral nerves or to the central nervous system itself), psychogenic pain (pain not due to past disease or injury or any visible sign of damage inside or outside the nervous system).

Is there any treatment?

Medications, acupuncture, local electrical stimulation, and brain stimulation, as well as surgery, are some treatments for chronic pain. Some physicians use placebos, which in some cases has resulted in a lessening or elimination of pain. Psychotherapy, relaxation and medication therapies, biofeedback, and behavior modification may also be employed to treat chronic pain.

What is the prognosis?

Many people with chronic pain can be helped if they understand all the causes of pain and the many and varied steps that can be taken to undo what chronic pain has done. Scientists believe that advances in neuroscience will lead to more and better treatments for chronic pain in the years to come.

What research is being done?

Clinical investigators have tested chronic pain patients and found that they often have lower-than-normal levels of endorphins in their spinal fluid. Investigations of acupuncture include wiring the needles to stimulate nerve endings electrically (electro acupuncture), which some researchers believe activates endorphin systems. Other experiments with acupuncture have shown that there are higher levels of endorphins in cerebrospinal fluid following acupuncture. Investigators are studying the effect of stress on the experience of chronic pain. Chemists are synthesizing new analgesics and discovering painkilling virtues in drugs not normally prescribed for pain (National Institutes of Health, 2008).

Most physicians in dealing with patients with chronic pain syndrome will either shrug and say "I can't help you" or recommend a referral to a psychiatrist. The patients and their families, often having dealt with the suffering and destruction of their lives for years, however, are desperate. They experiment with all forms of alternative medicine and, increasingly search the web for resources, even forming their own organizations and web sites (e.g. see: http://www.theacpa.org/default.asp).

South Park, like many other small rural hospitals, has faced dwindling occupancy and underutilized surgical suites as more aggressive marketing by larger urban medical centers siphoned off an increasing share of profitable surgical cases, and better roads allowed access to those centers. Reimbursement incentives increased competition for a shrinking inpatient hospital market by encouraging reduced length of stays and greater use of outpatient care while forcing hospitals to increase the volume of admissions and surgical procedures in order to cover their fixed costs.

Struggling to ensure its long term financial viability, South Park found a "rainmaker" that greatly increased its volume of profitable surgical care. In the process, however, the hospital slipped, unnoticed or ignored by internal and external quality review processes, into a medically and ethically questionable service line.

"The Rainmaker"

Dr. Rain is a neurological surgeon who has published extensively in his field and served on the faculty of a medical school. Dr. Rain developed a theory that many cases of chronic pain syndrome actually involved a congenital skull malformation that caused "posterior fossa compression" or, in deference to the doctor who first identified it, "Chiari malformation." He believed that other cases of chronic pain syndrome were caused by a too-narrow spinal canal, called "cervical spinal stenosis." Rain believed the reason these diagnoses were missed was because the malformations were so small that they went undetected. He felt that only careful review of an MRI by someone with the appropriate "skill" could identify them. His critics argued that there was nothing different in the MRIs that would distinguish them from normal ones and the cases in which there were real differences would be exceedingly rare. The advantage that these new and perhaps questionable diagnoses provided was that the surgical procedures now indicated became reimbursable by Medicare, Medicaid and private insurance carriers. Performing these operations for a diagnosis of chronic pain syndrome would not have been reimbursed. In the case of the "Chiari malformation," the indicated procedure was a "posterior fossa cranioectomy," This involved drilling and removing bone from the backs of people's skulls to "decompress" their brains. In the case of "cervical spinal stenosis," the procedure was a spinal laminectomy, which involved a similar drilling and removing of bone in the spinal column to "decompress" the spinal cord and central nervous system. Such procedures are complicated and potentially dangerous operations which are typically performed in a large tertiary care medical center.

In performing these procedures at the teaching hospital connected to the medical school where he was a faculty member, Rain soon found himself on a collision course with the chairman of his department and the medical school. Some patients had been thrilled with the results and some claimed that their condition had worsened. Four sued, claiming that unnecessary surgery had been performed at the medical school hospital. Doctors in the community had complained as well. In one letter, signed by

13 doctors, the doctors complained that patients were being victimized, "easy prey to someone who offers them a quick fix for a problem that does not have a quick fix." The chairman asked Rain to leave. Rain asked that an internal medical panel review the situation. The panel concluded by asking Rain how much money it would take for him to leave the University and a settlement was reached. Rain relocated to another state, took a "sabbatical" from practice, practiced briefly at large hospital where he raised similar concerns and then was recruited to South Park by its CEO.

The medical staff credentialing committee made quick work of accepting Rain to their staff, providing him with surgical privileges and then re-credentialing him after his first year on the hospital's medical staff. Rain was the only neurological surgeon on a staff composed mostly of family practice physicians, but no outside review of his credentials was requested. No phone calls or review of the news stories and related court documents was apparently done. In fact, no red flags were raised at all by his past activities. Thus, Rain's surgical practice grew quickly, spurred by internet sites that touted his services and success. Over the next three years, he performed a total of 650 crainiectomies and laminectomies, generating roughly $1.7 million dollars in gross revenues for his practice and $8 million dollars in gross revenues for the hospital each year. Rain offered little in the way of postoperative care for his patients, often limiting it to a single follow-up visit six weeks after surgery. Patients signed a standard "boilerplate" consent form for the surgery which gave no indication that there was anything potentially controversial or experimental about the treatment.

Perhaps goaded into action by a national TV show's coverage, in 2003, the State Medical Board initiated a hearing to determine whether Dr. Rain had engaged in unprofessional conduct by failing to conform to the standards of acceptable and prevailing medical practice in the state. The hearing investigated whether he had performed surgery that was not medically indicated, provided services in a manner that exploited the patients and failed to provide adequate postoperative care. The Board indefinitely suspended Dr. Rain's medical license for unprofessional conduct for doing unnecessary surgery. Dr. Rain's South Park privileges, as a result of this suspension, were automatically revoked.

Dr. Rain dismisses the situation as "all political" and insists that he will soon be vindicated and return to active practice. A well-known personal injury attorney has expanded his malpractice suit on behalf of a number of Dr. Rain's former patients to include the hospital.

Discussion

- What, if anything, went wrong with the process of controlling surgical practice in this case?
- Can an external voluntary professional review mechanism (Joint Commission on the Accreditation of Healthcare Organizations (JCAHO), Graduate Medical Education Accreditation Standards, Specialty Boards, etc.) correct this kind of behavior and the failure of internal quality assurance mechanisms in the face of such strong financial pressures?

Postscript

The malpractice case, now expanded to include additional plaintiffs, has yet to be settled or go to court. Dr. Rain, with some oversight restrictions in terms of second opinions, has his license back and is practicing at South Park. The administrator who served as the CEO of South Park during Dr. Rain's tenure has been promoted and now serves as the CEO of one of the larger hospitals in the system. He received a substantial raise with this promotion involving a salary and fringe benefit package that totaled $688,000 in 2004. Many hospital chains, mostly proprietary, operate with a similar approach, centralizing control of the financial side of operations and requiring financial benchmarks from the facilities that are members of their network, but largely insulating themselves from any control over a hospital's medical staff decisions concerning the credentialing process. Some would argue that this creates a perverse incentive that invites abuse.

Discussion

- How might the structure of medical staff organization in such hospital systems be changed to respond to the concerns of the plaintiffs?

4

Nursing: Where Is It Going and Why Does It Never Get There?

Nursing's Stunted Evolution

Better staffed, professionally trained nurses with higher morale reduce the chances of death, medical errors, re-admissions and delayed discharges in a hospital. Yet, morale and staffing problems have been a recurring theme in nursing (Institute of Medicine, 1996; Stanton, 2004; Nicken and Graves, 2005).

At the beginning of the 20th century, nurses were a small proportion of the healthcare workforce. 90% of it at that time consisted of physicians. The current occupational pyramid, with physicians accounting for less than 10% at the top and the complex division of labor with a diverse allied health workforce (everyone with clinical care responsibilities that are not physicians) beneath them did not exist. In many respects, nursing practice paralleled medical practice. Training took place in hospital schools of nursing where students did much of the nursing care for free as part of their training. Upon graduation, many became independent practitioners, allied with local visiting nurse associations, and contracting on a fee-for-service basis to care for the ill in their home.

Mirroring the industrialization that shifted manufacturing from cottage industry to factory, hospitals were transformed from marginalized sites on the periphery of the healthcare system to a central site of care for everyone. This shift coincided with a period of rapid medical advances and the hospital standardization efforts of the American College of

51

Surgeons. Both were shaped by the same idea that had transformed the manufacturing sector. Scientific management, the underlying paradigm that shaped all of these transformations, separated the planning of work from those doing it. This shift altered the role of nurses from that of independent craft persons/practitioners to part of an elaborate division of labor that, in theory, would most efficiently produce high quality hospital services but over which nurses had little effective control.

Two factors undermined nursing efforts to resist this shift in control. First, unlike medicine, nursing was unable to exercise full control over the production of nurses. Most nursing programs were originally operated by hospitals and designed to meet their needs and not the aspirations of the nursing profession. While independent university based nursing programs have gained influence, hospital based programs persist. The medical profession, through its professional associations and credentialing bodies, has been able to restrict production of physicians. Nursing, however, has never been as effective in controlling the supply of nurses by restricting employment to college degree trained registered nurses.

Second, shifts in the way nurses were paid undermined their independence. The major growth of hospital nursing employment took place in the 1930s and coincided with the economic shock of the Great Depression that dried up the demand for private duty nurses in people's homes. At the same time, the development of the third party payment mechanism bypassed nursing. Hospitals, facing the same payment problems of nurses providing home care, quickly developed "prepayment" plans (Blue Cross plans) that helped assure a reliable stream of income. Medicine followed suit and developed similar producer cooperative "prepayment" plans (Blue Shield plans). They were also successful in blocking forms of prepayment for their services that tended to undermine their control. Local medical societies fought bitter and successful battles against company and consumer sponsored group practice prepayment plans. They classified physicians that contracted with such plans as unethical and refused to accept them as members in their medical societies. Since hospital medical staffs were typically an extension of the local medical society and membership in good standing in the local medical society was a necessary condition for consideration for hospital privileges, they succeeded in making it impossible for those physicians to practice in their community. This delayed the development of managed care for almost fifty years. Nursing was never sufficiently organized to achieve similar successes and, with some minor accommodations, has never been able to directly bill health plans for their services. The "golden rule" in healthcare, as elsewhere, is that "those that control the gold rule."

The two cases presented in this chapter deal with struggles to overcome these barriers. Case 5 involves the effort to support nurse-midwives as independent practitioners in a hospital where they essentially served as its medical staff. Case 6 deals with the struggle to exert control over supply and the resulting difficulties in a region wracked by periodic shortages and surpluses. Both illustrate the continuing difficulties the nursing profession faces in getting the control it desires.

Case 5: Why Did Franklin Go Bankrupt?[6]

Marketing has always been a forbidden word in the hospital culture. It was undignified and tended to undermine the authority of the physician. With the shrinkage in demand for inpatient care, after the beginning of Diagnostic Related Group (DRG) payment to hospitals in 1984, the hospitals in the Philadelphia area discovered marketing with a vengeance. Cooper Medical Center in New Jersey advertised on a blimp at Eagles football games. Their campaign slogan was "We're on Your Side," a not particularly subtle effort to encourage New Jersey residents not to cross the bridges into Philadelphia for care. One North Philadelphia hospital set up an outreach office with a huge banner directly across the street from one of their competitors. All the big healthcare organizations in the area invested heavily in market research. Two perhaps obvious conclusions began to sink in: (1) women make most of the decisions about where family members get hospital care and (2) those choices are shaped primarily by where they received their maternity care and how satisfied they were with that experience. It became increasingly clear that part of the long term strategy for survival for most hospitals had to involve luring more maternity patients and increasing their satisfaction with the experience.

---

[6]The author served as a member of the board and executive committee and this account is based on his personal experiences and records.

Medical practice in Philadelphia has always been on the conservative side and this was certainly the case with maternity care. In the early 1980s, obstetricians still resisted allowing husbands into the delivery room or allowing the mother any choice in the manner of delivery. Now administrators had an interest in overcoming this resistance. Their attention focused on a facility in the city that had become a source of great irritation to Philadelphia's main stream obstetrical community: Booth Maternity Center, soon to be renamed John Franklin Maternity Hospital and Family Center.

The Loss of a Mission and the Invention of a New One

Booth Maternity Center had been operated by the Salvation Army in Philadelphia as a home for unwed mothers since 1896. It moved into its new three story facilities adjoining Saint Joseph University on City Line Ave in 1961. The new facility served as a place where pregnant teens from middle class families could be sent to avoid stigma, have their babies in secret, put them up for adoption and return to their communities. Yet, as that stigma lessened and as more pregnant teens chose either abortion or to keep their babies, this Level I maternity hospital with 18 beds, became increasingly empty.

Perhaps one of the strangest marriages of convenience in healthcare was consummated in 1971. The women's movement had emerged as a force to be reckoned with at the end of the 1960s. It focused on treatment of women by medical providers and stimulated a resurgence of interest in the nurse-midwifery model of maternity care. The midwifery approach rejected the mechanistic, physician controlled model of care. The mother was in control of the birth experience and should be assisted through all of its stages by a nurse-midwife. John Franklin, an obstetrician on the faculty at Jefferson, became a strong advocate for this approach to maternity care. He and four midwives approached the Salvation Army to use their now almost empty facility to offer this kind of care.

Booth Maternity Center emerged with a new burst of life and innovation. It became the national center of a movement aimed at radically altering maternity services by giving mothers full control in a safe environment. A jacuzzi was available for those who felt that this made labor more comfortable. Lamaze approaches to the birth experience were welcomed. Fathers were encouraged to participate. The facility struck a responsive chord with young expectant mothers and was soon operating at capacity, delivering more than 1,100 babies a year. People commuted from as far away as New York and Washington to be patients.

What the maternity center offered was something unique for that time in an organization that has never been successfully replicated. Nurse-midwives were full members of the medical staff of this Joint Commission of Healthcare Organizations (JCAHO) accredited hospital. Physicians were permitted to be members of the staff only in the role of supporting the midwives. The hospital cost for deliveries was low since the midwives themselves assisted the patient throughout the labor, delivery and recovery phases. Most parents participated in the prenatal and post discharge parenting classes that were offered in a carriage house which had been attractively renovated through the volunteer labor and financial contributions of Booth parents. Almost all parents participated in the first year birthday parties held for cohorts of babies, lively affairs that involved as many as 30 one-year-olds renewing acquaintances as their proud and amused parents looked on. The families that chose the maternity center were diverse. They came mostly from the Main Line and West Philadelphia. About 30% were Medicaid recipients, but patients also included University of Pennsylvania professors and partners at Center City law firms. The Philadelphia hospitals with large obstetric services watched the success and the decline of their own market share with growing envy.

Storm Clouds Loom with the Reorganization as John B. Franklin Maternity Hospital and Family Center

Beginning in 1984, the sunny days for the maternity center came to an end. Medicaid ceased to provide an all-inclusive rate, requiring the nurse-midwives to bill separately for their services as independent practitioners like physicians. The midwives who had been salaried employees of the maternity center now had to become independent entrepreneurs. It was an adjustment that was difficult for most, and it shifted concern about shared financial survival to concern about their own survival. Other hospitals began recruiting these and other nurse-midwives to set up their own "family centered" care programs. These hospitals began aggressively marketing their maternity services. They added new amenities to lure business, such as "free" candlelight steak and champagne dinners for the new parents. Franklin's market share sank and its deficits began to climb. The Salvation Army, which had been a willing partner in the more profitable times while the facility had been transformed into something unrelated to its core mission, chose to exit, announcing its intentions to close and sell the property.

A diverse assortment of individuals in the city came together, and with the help of several foundations and a complex series of financial arrangements, purchased the facility in 1986. It was renamed after one of the recently deceased founders of the midwifery based maternity program, John Franklin.

The Final Efforts to Save the Maternity Center

Most of 1987 was spent in marketing and fundraising efforts that met with some success. Outreach efforts to city health centers had resulted in some increase in registrations. After much debate about its potential impact on the cost and quality of care at Franklin, the staff medical bylaws were changed to allow for membership in the medical staff of physicians not serving in a supporting role to the midwives. The hope was to provide a new gynecological surgery and diagnostic care service line to generate additional revenues. A partnership with the Frontier Nursing Service (FNS) of Lexington, Kentucky was finalized, providing up to $2 million dollars in funds to assist in paying bills, marketing and investing in new equipment. FNS was established in 1925 to provide nurse practitioner based health services in the remote areas of Appalachia accessible only on horseback. They recruited adolescent volunteer horseback riders from the Philadelphia Main Line to deliver supplies. Fifty years later, this proved to have been a brilliant fundraising ploy. Some of these women now served on the FNS Board. They and others who had shared the same experiences in their youth had contributed part of their inherited family fortunes to generously endow the FNS. The FNS, however, was now struggling to revitalize its own mission. What had been remote areas of Appalachia in the 1930s were now crisscrossed with four lane highways, making more urban mainstream care accessible and reducing the volume of deliveries they needed to train the next generation of nurse-midwives. Franklin offered an ideal new site for such training.

In 1988, it became clear, however, these efforts were not going to be sufficient to revive Franklin. The hospital needed to find a healthcare organization in Philadelphia with the resources to acquire it and an appreciation of the potential contribution of the facility and its mission to their operations. In its monthly financial statements that year (which understated the magnitude of the problem), losses from operations were averaging about $125,000 a month. The fund balance was losing that same amount every month and was listed as −$1.585 million. In short, Franklin owed substantially more than it was worth. Additional loans were out of the question. After unsuccessful negotiations with several other potential purchasers, a draft deal was worked out with the neighboring Osteopathic Hospital. The deal, however, required that the Salvation Army agree to forego a portion of the funds they were due. Their obstinate refusal meant they would lose *all* of the funds they were due. It also sealed the fate of the hospital.

In January 1989, Franklin Maternity Hospital and Family Center filed for Chapter 11 bankruptcy protection and the facility began an orderly closure. As indicated in the newspaper headline and editorial below, it was a traumatic experience (Figs. 4.1, 4.2). Several hundred women arrived the day after the announcement with children in tow, in part to participate in a spontaneous protest and in part to show their children where they were born, and to have a last look at a place that had played such an important part in their lives. While the closing of a community hospital is always mourned by its community, perhaps no facility in Philadelphia that has closed since or will close in the future, is likely to generate such an outpouring of grief from its former patients. The facility was sold at a Sheriff's auction in June to Saint Joseph's University and later converted into a dormitory. The facility's staff was scattered across the city to facilities that now embraced many of the ideas concerning care pioneered at the maternity center. That staff continues as an underground network whose participants still reflect with nostalgia about the special place that Franklin was and what was lost.

My **Crummy** Valentine
page 5

CITY PAPER

The

Philadelphia's Free Weekly Newspaper • February 10-17, 1989 • No. 235

Death
of a *Birth*
Center

How market forces

Fig. 4.1.   The Death of a Birth Center (City Paper, 1989).

Discussion

- The Franklin bankruptcy was largely driven by the decision of many of the larger hospital systems to enter the niche maternity market occupied by Franklin. Why were they interested in developing and marketing this new "product line" of nurse- midwife based "family centered" maternity services, in spite of the resistance to the idea on the part of some their obstetricians?

- Some healthcare critics argue for the creation of more "competitive markets." They say it is the only way to reduce costs and improve quality. One could argue that the case of Franklin proves that such markets work. In response to competitive pressures, other hospital marketing efforts responded to the challenge posed by Franklin and changing consumer preferences. From your perspective, did the market really work?

The Philadelphia Inquirer

An Independent Newspaper

SAM S. McKEEL
Publisher and Chairman

EUGENE L. ROBERTS JR.
Executive Editor and President

DAVID R. BOLDT
Editor of the Editorial Page

Monday, February 6, 1989   Page 10

EDITORIALS

Franklin Maternity is a great loss

The Jan. 25 article on the closing of the Franklin Maternity Hospital implies some overly comforting conclusions to your readers. Franklin, the article implies, was a victim of its own success.

Family-centered and midwifery-based obstetrical services initiated at that hospital 15 years ago are now widely available in the Delaware Valley.

Certainly there is no overall shortage of obstetrical beds, as occupancy statistics and the intense advertising campaigns of some local hospitals can attest. The market is working. Other than those directly affected, why should anyone else really care?

First, we are losing a distinctly different and successful social experiment in obstetric care. Franklin, on whose board I sit, was the only hospital in the country where midwives have full staff privileges. (Indeed, a lengthy debate among the clinical staff preceded allowing physicians on the staff to practice independently of midwives, fearing that it would undermine the quality of care.)

As one recently published study documented, it produced healthier babies and mothers than a comparable population receiving care at a medical school facility with a fine obstetrical service. It also accomplished this at less than half the cost.

Perhaps even more unusual, it was an alternative model of care that recruited and appealed to mothers of all social backgrounds. A Franklin patient was as likely to be, in spite of the lack of plush carpeted surroundings, a partner in a Center City law firm or a Penn professor as a welfare mother. They shared a common experience and a desire to have a degree of control over that experience. That control, glossy advertising brochures to the contrary, remains more elusive in other settings.

Second, we are losing the only hospital facility in the Delaware Valley exclusively committed by its mission, the nature of its programs and its geographic location to mothers and their babies and to reducing infant-mortality rates and the staggering costs of premature births. Those rates in Philadelphia and, particularly, in parts of Franklin's service area are among the worst in the country.

The city may have plenty of obstetrical beds and enough costly neonatal intensive-care units. But it doesn't have enough of the midwives and counselors such as those in Franklin's adolescent pregnancy program fighting for their clients, hassling them when they miss prenatal appointments, supporting them as they try to finish their education, and helping them, in spite of overwhelming odds, to become what it is more difficult than anything else to become, a good parent.

It may be that the Philadelphia community is not prepared to support a free-standing facility such as Franklin. It is clear that strictly as a business venture, it can't survive on its own in the current environment.

The bricks and mortar and other physical assets are not important, but the vision and the programs deserve to be saved and nurtured. Their loss should be unacceptable to everyone.

David Barton Smith
Swarthmore

Fig. 4.2. The Loss of Franklin (The Philadelphia Enquirer, 1989).

Postscript

The bankruptcy of Franklin came at the peak of growth of the family centered maternity care movement. Since then, the tide in obstetrical care has tended to ebb in the opposite direction. Unable to absorb the rising malpractice costs, fewer nurse-midwives care for deliveries in Philadelphia. Ironically in view of the demise of Franklin, obstetrical care itself has shifted from a service that hospitals aggressively competed for to one that, left to their own devices, they would rather eliminate.

Obstetrics as a physician specialty choice has increasingly combined the worst of all possible worlds — the higher malpractice costs of high-risk surgical specialties and the lower income potential of primary care practices. Not surprisingly, the number of medical graduates choosing to go into obstetrics has dropped by nearly 50% since 1980. Philadelphia has been particularly affected by the spiraling malpractice costs with the number of obstetricians declining by 27% in the last decade (Bishop, 2007).

Malpractice insurance costs in Philadelphia jumped to $134,335 per obstetrician in 2003, precipitating a crisis for hospital obstetrical services (Mello, Student *et al.*, 2007). Hospitals wishing to keep obstetrical services had to help subsidize these malpractice insurance costs and, in some cases, directly employ their obstetricians. Obstetricians increasingly practiced defensive medicine. They insisted that the hospitals where they practiced provide all the latest in costly technology, including neonatal intensive care units. One of the goals of nurse-midwifery based obstetric care was to reduce the rates of cesarean sections. While cesarean sections, from the perspective of obstetricians, are more lucrative, less time consuming and less prone to malpractice risks than normal deliveries, most would argue that they should be a last resort in terms of the health of the mother and baby. Yet nationally, c-section rates have climbed from 22% to 28% in the last decade, and are now at the highest level in history (Menacker, 2005). In turn, hospital obstetrical services have generated increasing losses. Hospitals have always lost some money on obstetrical care, but now they were losing more and it was harder to offset these losses with profits in other areas. In addition, these obstetrical care losses could no longer be justified as a way of marketing or attracting patients. Increasingly, it was the health plans that guided patients to hospitals through selective competitive contracting for services rather than the choices of consumers. Managers were not as concerned about building hospital loyalty though obstetric care. As a result, in the last decade 14 hospitals in the Philadelphia area have ceased to provide obstetrical services. Of these, seven hospitals with obstetrical services closed and seven others closed their OB units (Bishop, 2007). Expectant mothers in Philadelphia now face a shortage in obstetrical services with fewer choices, more crowded conditions, and more defensive, impersonalized care.

Discussion

- Is the shift in OB care appropriate? If not, what steps would be necessary to reverse this trend?

Case 6: How Should Healthcare Organizations Respond to the Nursing "Shortage"?[7]

In 1996, the Pennsylvania Economy League (PEL) published what was widely considered a definitive assessment: the Philadelphia region faced a growing surplus of Registered Nurses (RN) (Pennsylvania Economy League, 1996). They had done their homework and the conclusion was a persuasive one. Their extensive statistical analysis of trends in supply and demand had been supplemented by interviews with more than 90 regional experts. Furthermore, their assessment was consistent with widely held national views about the impact of the managed care transformation on the healthcare system. The PEW Health Professions Commission had just completed a national review of healthcare workforce needs and its

---

[7]This case distills the analysis that previously appeared in Smith, D. B. and W. Aarronson (2003). "The Perils of Healthcare Workforce Forecasting: A Caste Study of the Philadelphia Metropolitan Area." *Journal of Healthcare Management* **48**(2): 99–11 and in a report done under contract with the Pennsylvania Center for Health Careers, Pennsylvania Workforce Investment Board Smith, D. B. (2004). An Assessment of the Supply and Demand for Registered and Licensed Practical Nurses in the Commonwealth of Pennsylvania. Philadelphia, Department of Risk, Insurance and Healthcare Management, Temple University: 1–34.

conclusions paralleled those of PEL (The Pew Health Professions Commission, 1994; The Pew Health Professions Commission, 1995; The Pew Health Professions Commission, 1995). The Pew analysis concluded that there was an oversupply of medical specialists, a potential surplus of hospital trained nurses and a need for a fundamental shift in training to reflect a reconfigured and downsized hospital sector.

The PEL report noted that the oversupply of nurses was likely to continue to increase, as a result of a decline in hospital employment. Nursing graduates were having trouble finding work. The traditional acute care positions that nurses sought were becoming scarce and graduates were being forced to accept lower-skill positions in hospitals or nursing homes before being "promoted" to RN positions. Other nurses were resorting to less conventional forms of employment. For example, some were, as hospital managers described it, going over to "the dark side" and serving as case managers for health insurance plans. Others were taking positions as clinical trial supervisors for pharmaceutical companies.

While hospital employment in the Philadelphia region almost doubled between 1975 and 1992, it then began a dramatic three year decline (Smith and Aarronson, 2003). The increasing dominance of selective managed care contracting drove harder bargains with hospitals in a market that was generally viewed as having excess capacity. Underlying this shift was an economic downturn in the region in the early 1990s that forced the state Medicaid program and private health plans, feeling the pressure from employer purchasers, into tougher bargaining positions with the hospitals. Hospitals had to trim their budgets and, in the short run, the main place that such cuts could be taken was in nurse staffing. Nursing staff represents more than half the cost of running a hospital and many of the other costs such as malpractice insurance and debt repayment were impossible to cut and increasing. Headlines in the Philadelphia papers during this period announced nursing staff layoffs at many of the hospitals in the region. Many other hospitals cut staff less publicly and painfully through attrition and hiring freezes.

Clearly, at least for the foreseeable future, there were plenty of nurses to go around. Or were there?

Beginning in 2000, health service providers in the Philadelphia region began to face a growing shortage. A consortium of hospitals and educational institutions in Greater Philadelphia created the "Life Science

Career Alliance" to encourage students to enter the nursing profession. Now there were nursing vacancies that could not be filled and the vacancy rate was growing. Hospitals were falling back on using overtime, part-timers, and per diem staff and hospital float pools to fill the gaps. In the process, the old gentlemen's understanding between hospitals about keeping the salaries of their nursing staff comparable broke down. Hospitals would lure nurses away from other hospitals in the region with signing bonuses and salaries that now edged close to that of starting physicians. Seeing young and inexperienced new nurses surpass them in earnings and feeling unappreciated, loyal long time nurses at hospitals left and sought better earnings at other hospitals. Reflecting the national scope of this shift, some nurses became "traveling nurses" visiting attractive areas of the country and combining brief stints of highly remunerative employment with vacations. Some hospitals in Philadelphia tried to aggressively reinvigorate their nursing schools and others financed recruitment in Ireland, the Philippines and South Africa. Hospitals in other areas of the country, such as North-Carolina, began to pay for recruitment in Philadelphia. Nursing had been turned into a chaotic global sellers' market.

A new series of reports heralded the beginning of a nursing shortage of epic proportions (Nursing Institute, 2001; The Hospital Association of Pennsylvania, 2001; National Center for Workforce Analysis, 2004). The number of admissions, as well as the number of graduates from registered nursing programs in Pennsylvania, had dropped almost 50% between 1995 and 2000. Only about half of the registered nurses residing in the Philadelphia region in 2000 were currently providing direct patient care. The rest sought employment elsewhere, left the workforce to raise families or retired. The National Center for Workforce Analysis forecasted increasing demand for nursing care for an aging population and declining supply from an even more rapidly aging nurse workforce (National Center for Workforce Analysis, 2004). It estimated that the shortage of nurses would grow to almost 30%, (nationally a shortage 808,416 full-time equivalent RNs and, for Pennsylvania, a shortage of 40,381 full-time equivalent RNs) by 2020 (National Center for Workforce Analysis, 2004). Philadelphia area and state reports echoed these concerns, arguing for a coordinated approach to recruit nursing students, expand nursing programs, and create conditions that would reduce the attrition of nurses from nursing.

Discussion

- As a member of a task force reviewing this problem, what recommendations would you make for addressing the immediate problem?
- More than half the nursing workforce in hospitals in the Philadelphia region is temporary or part-time. Hospital medical staff consists of volunteers and are sporadic in their attention to hospital affairs. At best, physicians devote less than a day a month to hospital matters unrelated to their direct care responsibilities and most have staff privileges in at least two hospitals. Continuous quality improvement first developed in industrial settings where employees had a full-time, long term commitment to the organization. Is it realistic to transplant such models to these kinds of settings which involve a far more complex production process? What would you propose?

Postscript

Nursing shortages are not a new problem and the cycles of shortages and surpluses of nurses existed for at least sixty years before the events described in this case and seem likely to persist after them. The shortage tends to appear during periods of high general employment and disappear when unemployment rates increase. In good economic times, nurses tend to be attracted to jobs in other sectors and in bad economic times, these options become more limited. In addition, many nurses provide the second income in a family. In good economic times, they may opt out of the work force and in bad times, they may return as the sole bread winner. Helping to exacerbate these cycles, healthcare providers in good economic times tend to benefit from more generous health plan payments and can afford to expand nurse staffing. In bad economic times they face more frugal payments and have to cut back on staffing. The first notable shortage took place in the 1940s during World War II and in Philadelphia, this helped spur the racial integration of hospital nursing staffs. Another shortage prior to the one in the case took place in the late 1980s and disappeared in the early 1990s as unemployment rates rose.

These mirror image boom and bust cycles of supply and demand are further exacerbated by the lag between when individuals decide to prepare for a nursing career and when they actually enter the workforce. For example, faced with headlines about nursing layoffs and reports such as the one produced by PEL about the oversupply of nurses, applications and admissions to nursing programs in Pennsylvania dropped by half. Faced with reports and headlines in the early 2000s about the demand for nurses, the bonuses and highly competitive salaries that graduates were getting, the number of nursing school applicants expanded. By 2003, admissions to nursing programs in Pennsylvania had exceeded the 1995 high and they have continued to increase (Smith, 2004). Nursing schools expanded to accommodate this increasing demand and new nursing programs were created. Beginning in 2008, the perception of most observers in the Philadelphia area is that the nursing shortage is pretty much over. The economic difficulties that began in 2008 seem likely to return us again to the "oversupply" conditions described in the first part of this case.

Discussion

- What steps would you take to ensure that the efforts to align nursing supply with demand do not again "miss the mark"?

5

Financing: How Gold Rules

Following the Money

Paying for the costs of illness has never been like paying for other products or services. A small part of any population accounts for a large proportion of its health expenditures. For example, in any given year in the U.S., 1% of the population accounts for 25–29% of all health expenditures, while 50% accounts for only about 3% and close to 17% will have no expenditures at all (Wu and Machlin, 2004). Age is the best predictor of how much individuals will spend on healthcare, but in the over 65 years of age population, Medicare expenditures are only slightly less concentrated with 1% of the beneficiaries accounting for 20% of the expenditures (Riley, 2007). Since illness reduces the ability to earn income, that 1% of the U.S. population with the highest expenditures is also the group (with the possible exception of the elderly who have Medicare) least likely to be able to afford to pay for the costs of an illness or for the health insurance that would help protect them from these costs.

Commercial insurance companies were latecomers to the health insurance market. Not until the late 1940s did these companies start to develop any interest in this market. Why bother? Those most in need of such policies were the least likely to be able to afford them. In addition, healthcare expenditures are not the rare, catastrophic, and un-anticipatable single event insurance companies traditionally liked to underwrite. Insurance companies also did not like the idea of the purchasers of insurance knowing more about the likelihood of incurring expenses than they did and not being a party to the decisions of patients and their doctors about treatment inevitably influenced by the kind of insurance coverage a person has. It presented what insurance companies call a "moral hazard."

In the United States as in other countries, protecting people from illness and healthcare expenses started out being something very different. Local lodges and fraternal orders in the 19th century provided assistance to their members who were victims of accidents or illness. At first, members just passed a hat to take up a collection for an unfortunate colleague. They would also donate food and provide assistance in carrying out household chores. These mutual aid associations evolved into funds to which members were expected to make regular payments. The idea behind these sickness funds was that "we" whoever that was (a church congregation, fraternal order, new immigrant group or recently emancipated slaves) are all in this together and we will take care of each other, just the way we would for a sick family member. It was a moral obligation, not a product one could choose to purchase. One way that this was done was to contract with a physician to provide care for all of their members. They would negotiate a flat rate per member per year with a physician, an early version of pre-payment (Rosen, 1977). Local medical societies felt threatened by such contracting and fought against what they called "the lodge practice of medicine," refusing to accept physicians with such practices as members. Medicine viewed the direct fee-for-service relationship between a doctor and a patient as an essential, sacrosanct part of the doctor-patient relationship and also feared the impact of lodge medicine arrangements on their own ability to earn a living. Hospitals, however, picked up on this approach during the Great Depression and began creating voluntary "community" hospital insurance plans. These plans would collect funds from members in much the same way, either through volunteers at the work site or going door to door. These voluntary plans evolved into the local Blue Cross plans that now occupy a large share of the private health insurance market in the United States. It was not initially considered a business; it was just a way of taking care of those who fell ill. Community members felt responsible for looking after each other. This moral obligation was, as some have described, "the soul" of such insurance (Stone, 1993).

Similar arrangements evolved in other countries into national health plans, assuring universal health insurance coverage. It seemed like a natural, logical progression. The "soul" of the sickness funds was expanded to ensure that all citizens were included. Yet, this never happened in the United States. Health insurance in the United States began to follow a different direction after World War II. President Truman's national health insurance proposal went down to defeat in 1948. Private insurance companies entered the market drawn by the rapid expansion of employer-sponsored health insurance. Most commercial companies at first just viewed it as a "loss leader," a way of getting their foot in the door so that they could sell the employer other lines of insurance. Their entry, however, brought disruptive fundamental change in how health insurance was financed and in the philosophy underlying it. The cornerstone of the previously developed local non-profit plans was "community rating." That meant everybody paid the same amount regardless of how costly that coverage might be for the plan. The 50% who accounted for 3% of the costs paid the same as the 1% that accounted for as much as 29% of the cost. It was just a simple extension of the idea used to create the early sickness funds. From the perspective of the commercial insurance companies, however, this made no sense. They felt premiums, like any other insurance product, should be based on "actuarial fairness." That is, your premiums should be related to your experience or risk. An employer with a young and healthy workforce should pay less than one with older and sicker employees. For the salespersons of the commercial plans, it was like taking candy from babies. It was easy to sell policies to low risk employer groups at a rate much lower than the overall community rate. As a result of what the community-rated plans regarded as "cream-skimming" by the commercials, the premium costs in the community-rated plans sky rocketed. They were left covering only the employer groups with the most costly experience. The only way the non-profit community plans could survive was to convert to experience rating too and compete on an equal footing with the commercial plans. Somewhere in that process, the "soul" or rationale of the original health and sickness funds got lost. Health insurance became a commercial insurance business. As a result, those that needed it the most were left to the government to insure or became uninsured. The United States has been struggling to address the social and economic consequences of this ever since.

Physicians and hospitals, just like the non-profit plans, did what they had to do to survive, and, as a consequence, reshaped the system. Non-profit hospitals talk defensively about "no margin, no mission" and sometimes with resignation about the "golden rule" (those that have the gold rule), but they had become a business and not a charity. It was, however, not just a matter of "following the money" as Deep Throat (FBI Deputy Director W. Mark Felt) advised Woodward and Bernstein in the Watergate investigation of the Nixon White House. Providers had to understand how the money was packaged and the best approaches to getting as much of it as possible.

Hospitals and other providers go through the process of doing this every year. They align their strategy with the way they get paid when they pull together their budgets. They figure out how best to maximize their revenues and minimize their costs. If, for example, hospitals were forced into being paid a flat rate per admission instead of their actual costs per day, as they did when the Medicare Prospective payment began in the mid-1980s, length of stay would drop and patients would get discharged "quicker and sicker." Pay obstetricians twice as much for a c-section that takes less time than normal deliveries and you get more c-sections. Pay hospitals more than it actually costs for open heart surgery and, lacking other controls, you get more hospitals doing open heart surgery and pronouncing it as one of their "centers of excellence."

Patients, of course, go through a similar set of calculations. Sure, no one does comparison shopping on prices as they are being rushed to the hospital emergency room suffering from a suspected heart attack. At the point of service, particularly for critical services around a potentially life threatening condition, price is no object. Everyone, however, looks at their paycheck stub and winces at how much is cut out of their gross pay to cover their health insurance premiums. Given a choice of health insurance plans that appear roughly the same, they will take the one that cuts the least out of their paycheck. Similarly, if deductibles and co-payments are raised, they will go to their doctor less frequently and only when they are really worried, even if these delays may eventually result in higher costs for the health plan. In addition, if a new health plan option offers lower premiums in exchange for restricting where you can get care, healthier subscribers with fewer health worries are more likely to switch. As best they can, with the available options, consumers will maximize what they get and minimize their costs. For example, if employees have the choice between a managed care plan that offers comprehensive outpatient coverage and a more traditional policy that just offers coverage of hospitalization costs, with no waiting period for maternity coverage, the managed care plan will enroll a lot more pregnant women. If a plan does not cover the cost of a drug needed to manage a chronic condition, the individual will try to find a plan that does and their previous plan will be saved the costs involved in caring for someone with such a chronic condition.

Health plans are aware of all these things about their providers and enrollees. They too, within the market and regulatory constraints that they face, will try to maximize their revenues and minimize their costs. In essence, they play a four dimensional high stakes chess game with their (1) providers, (2) enrollees, (3) purchasers and (4) competitors. Within this game, as it has evolved, there have been some highly talented players. This chapter describes the games of two such players. Case 7 describes Len Abramson, who entered the game with a government loan and left 25 years later selling his health insurance company for $8.3 billion. Case 8 deals with a small team in the state Medicaid program. They leveraged Medicaid dollars, turning the health establishment in the Philadelphia Metropolitan Area on its head.

Case 7: Len Abramson and U.S. Healthcare
— By Robert Uris[8]

Background

With community rating abandoned in the employer based insurance market, the key calculation that health plans sweated over was price. You could beat out your competitors in this market if you could offer your plan with the same package of benefits to an employer at a lower price or more benefits at the same price. The benefits in these early plans, however, were typically limited to covering the costs of hospitalizations. In the 1950s, some began to realize that it might be possible to cut the price by changing the way providers of services were paid. Commercial insurance plans provided

---

[8] Robert Uris was a hospital administrator in Philadelphia during much of the period described in this case. His account has been edited to fit in with the style and content of the other cases presented in this book.

indemnity policies that would cover a portion of the fees for physician and hospital services billed to the insured. Typically, such policies had a "deductible" — an amount the insured had to pay before the insurance would begin to pay — and a "coinsurance," a portion of the remaining bill for which the insured was responsible. It was a policy contracted between the insured or their employer and the insurance carrier. Hospitals and physicians were not involved. The major competitive advantage that traditional non-profit plans, the Blue Cross and Blue Shield plans, had over the commercials was that they negotiated directly with providers and received services at a discounted rate, but they still paid on a fee-for-service basis.

In a few areas of the country, an alternative form of payment, prepaid group practices began to account for a significant share of the market. Prepaid group practices provided a service benefit that included a comprehensive package of preventive, primary, specialty and hospital services for a flat rate per year. It was not a new idea. The fraternal orders and lodges at the turn of the 20th century had done this, negotiating a flat rate with individual physicians to care for their members. This shifted the risk on to the physicians who were now paid the same flat rate no matter how many services they provided or how sick some of the lodge members became. This approach, applied to an organized group of physicians, had been used to develop a few prepaid group practice plans. For example, the Puget Sound Cooperative Prepaid Group Practice plan emerged out of a cooperative community effort to save a bankrupt hospital and the Kaiser-Permanente Prepaid Group Practice Plan developed out of the efforts of physician Sidney Garfield to sell medical services to remote construction sites of the Kaiser-Permanente Corporation. Local medical societies were just as hostile to these prepaid group practices as they had been to the physicians who had earlier engaged in the "lodge practice" of medicine. Doctors employed by these prepaid practice plans were refused membership in local medical societies and privileges at local hospitals because, since they engaged in this form of practice, they were "unworthy in character and matters of professional ethics." As a result, many of these prepaid practices had to acquire or build their own hospitals. These plans relied on a salaried medical staff to provide care. The physician leaders of these plans argued that this was the right way to practice medicine and only in such a comprehensive integrated system could the best quality of care be provided. The social visionaries who helped create these plans believed that it gave physicians the freedom to practice medicine by working cooperatively with colleagues so that all the resources of modern medicine could be brought to bear in treating patients unconstrained by the patients' ability to pay for it.

In the 1950s, however, it began to be clear to these plans that the cost of their more comprehensive services was substantially less than the cost of more traditional, more limited fee-for-service coverage. Hospitalizations are the major component of the costs of any health plan and the rates of hospitalization in these prepaid group practices were substantially lower. "Not only do we provide better quality of care," they now argued, "but we save money doing it." The reason for this, they argued was that they had an incentive to keep people healthy and out of hospitals by providing good preventive and primary care. "Fee-for-service is an irrational incentive," they argued.

It was not, however, quite that simple. One of the principles insisted upon by these prepaid group practice plans was that people had to be free to choose this form of care and to have the option of remaining in a more traditional fee-for-service plan. Making patients use a closed panel of physicians they did not want to use, they argued, did not make for a good doctor-patient relationship or for good medical care. It also, possibly inadvertently, resulted in some cream-skimming at the expense of the more traditional fee-for-service plans. (The commercial indemnity plans had done this and now the non-profit prepaid group practices were beating them at their own game!) An employee faced with a choice between a more traditional fee-for-service hospitalization plan and the more comprehensive service staff model prepaid practice plan, made perfectly rational choices. If they had a long established relationship with a private practice physician (e.g. they tended to be older and have a serious medical condition that they were worried about), they were more reluctant to sever their existing medical ties and join a prepaid group practice plan. If they were younger, relatively healthy, had not really established a strong relationship with an existing medical practice and their medical needs were more likely to be limited to preventive and primary care services, they were more likely to choose the prepaid group practice plan. The result was beneficial risk selection into the group practice plan and adverse risk selection into the more traditional plans.

Partly as a result of risk selection, the prepaid plans were able to offer more benefits for the same premium of the traditional plans. Often, because premiums of the more traditional plans did not adequately reflect this adverse risk selection, the premiums had to be raised. Employers typically chose to take responsibility for covering the costs of the lower cost option and the employee that chose the higher cost plan had to make up the difference. The difference in out-of-pocket costs made the prepaid group practice plan more attractive. It also increased the differential risk selection into the two plans. One of the lessons health insurers have learned is that "that the price sets the experience." Now that employees had to pay out of their pockets for the price difference between two plans, they really had to have a reason to stick with the traditional plan and that was often that they or one of their family members had a costly acute or chronic condition and were afraid to switch providers in the midst of these medical problems.

Employers and public policy makers, however, were slow to learn two key lessons from the prepaid practice experience. The first lesson was that a portion of the "cost savings" from prepaid group practices flowed not from the incentives they provided for better management of people's care, but from the beneficial risk selection. The second lesson was that a lot of the savings that employers and public policy makers thought they would get from switching most of the population they were responsible for into prepaid group practice plans would be illusory.

These lessons, however, never quite got translated into the broader policy arena. Concern about controlling the cost of health care in the United States became a central concern in public debate in the 1970s and prepaid group practice, now promoted as "Health Maintenance Organizations" (HMOs), became the magic bullet. The federal HMO Act of 1973 was designed to encourage a shift towards HMOs.

The HMO Act in 1973 was a fateful watershed in the development of pre-paid group practice. The ambiguity of what an HMO really was and the promise it seemed to hold of reducing costs enabled broad bipartisan support. Paul Elwood, credited with coining the term "Health Maintenance Organization," was a persuasive evangelist. Who could be against something that saved money by keeping people healthy? As President Nixon noted in his State of the Union Address in 1972:

> *The Health Maintenance Organization Act ... is an essential tool*
> *for helping doctors deliver care more effectively and more effi-*
> *ciently with a greater emphasis on prevention and early treatment.*
> *By working to keep our people healthy instead of treating us only*
> *when we are sick, Health Maintenance Organizations can do a*
> *great deal to help us reduce medical costs*
>
> *(Nixon, 1972).*

While the evidence of real health promotion and cost savings was unconvincing, the argument helped sell the legislation. The original act provided $375 million in grants and loans for the planning and development of non-profit HMOs and, more importantly, required employers providing health insurance coverage to more than 25 employees to provide an HMO option if available.

The most fateful decision, lost in the details of the legislation and in subsequent amendments, however, was to permit independent practice associations (IPAs) to qualify as HMOs. IPAs are not prepaid group practices. However, medical associations had the ear of the Nixon Administration and supported their inclusion. IPAs were originally set up by local medical societies to fight against the threat of encroachment by Kaiser and other prepaid group practices. It enabled local physicians to continue to practice independently in fee-for-service practices, yet collectively offer an alternative service based prepayment plan. The advantage IPAs had was that they did not require much capital to set up. All you had to do was get the doctors to agree to participate. However, most of them quickly got into financial trouble. The early medical society sponsored IPAs were open to all medical society members, often continued to pay participating physicians on a fee-for-service basis and had little in the way of effective utilization controls. You could, in theory, control costs in an IPA by being selective about the practices you allowed to participate and by creating controls and incentives to rein in use of inpatient hospital care and costly diagnostic and specialty services. However, at least up until the 1970s, nobody had been effective in doing this with a collection of independent practices that were financially independent from the plan. The IPAs also faced an even more formidable barrier to their financial survival — adverse risk selection. Enrollees were offered all the benefits in terms of coverage of outpatient services of a prepaid group practice without having to change their doctor. This was a much more attractive deal for those that saw their physician frequently (e.g. higher risk). In many cases, doctors would exacerbate this adverse risk selection by advertising their IPA in their waiting rooms and personally encouraging their patients to enroll. In terms of risk selection, this was equivalent to aggressively marketing auto insurance in a body repair shop. You do not want to sell auto insurance only to those who have accidents and you do not want to sell health insurance only to those who are sick.

The new law caught the attention of Leonard Abramson, a 41-year-old Pennsylvania pharmacist. He quickly figured a way to fix the fatal flaws in the IPA model and proceeded to take full advantage of the initial HMO Act funding.

Abramson's Wild IPA Ride

While most of the "experts" assumed that the newly developed IPAs would all flop, Abramson saw in the Philadelphia area market a perfect opportunity to launch a successful one. It had an excess capacity of physicians and hospital beds. Why not selectively contract, negotiating discounts from physicians and hospitals? One could also make the business risk-free by shifting the risk onto primary care physicians. The premium could be divided into three pieces. One piece would provide a monthly payment to the physician, who assumed responsibility for an enrollee as their primary care physician and gatekeeper. The other two pieces would serve as pools for paying specialty and hospital care. If there was anything left over in these two pools at the end of the year, the primary care physician would get a share of it as a bonus. This basic model was refined over time to include quality of care bonuses to help detract growing criticism of an incentive system designed to discourage specialty and hospital use. The key was to keep the price the same as the traditional Blue Cross and Blue Shield coverage that provided more limited benefits. As enrollment in the plan grew, it could bargain more effectively for discounts from the hospitals and physicians, exchanging the promised larger volume and, consequently, more income for deeper discounts.

Abramson's IPA, Health Maintenance Organization of PA (HMO/PA), was structured differently from the earlier IPAs. It was completely separate from the physicians who would serve as providers and viewed its relationship with them as an "arms length" contractual one. The local medical society was certainly viewed as an adversary. Abramson would pick and choose whichever physicians helped him achieve his goals, weeding out those whose practice patterns and use of hospital and specialized services exceeded benchmarks in the contract renewal process. The key was to avoid the adverse risk selection that was typical in the physician sponsored IPAs. He selected practices in newer, growing suburban areas and younger primary care physicians in these areas who were beginning to grow their practices and were willing to accept modest "per member per month" prepaid fees. By concentrating on physicians that served these younger, more affluent and growing suburban areas and by selecting practices that fit the low cost practice profile he desired, Abramson avoided the problem of "adverse selection" and succeeded in doing some "cream skimming" of his own, replicating the experience of the earlier prepaid group practices.

Established as a non-profit organization in 1976, Abramson took advantage of the federal development funds available through the HMO Act of 1973. In 1977, HMO/PA qualified for certification and funding under the new Federal law. Enrollment is critical to the financial survival of an HMO. In the early years, with fewer than 20,000 members, HMO/PA had yet to break even. It was a "chicken and egg" type of problem. On the one hand, new members were not interested in enrolling if family physicians near where they lived were not participants in HMO/PA. On the other hand, local physicians were not interested in taking the relatively modest payments offered by HMO/PA unless doing so would substantially increase the volume of patients and profitability of their practice. HMO/PA faced a daunting challenge.

Yet, with a mixture of luck and genius that would mark the rest of his career, Abramson was always in the right place at the right time. The local Blue Cross plan had long dominated the Philadelphia area employer health insurance market with more than a 70% market share. Originally formed by the area hospitals, a kind of "producers' cooperative" health plan, it had yet to transition to a more arms length and adversarial relationship with the hospitals. The regional hospital association negotiated the contracts collectively for all the hospitals with Blue Cross. It was the way these contracts had always been done and it never occurred to the Blue Cross executives that, through a strategy of dividing and conquering the hospitals by individually negotiating contracts, they could cut better deals. They also shared the assumptions and values of the local hospital and physician culture that HMOs were not an appropriate way to finance care and would never catch on in the Philadelphia market. As a result, like a frightened ostrich, Blue Cross stuck its head in the sand and did not enter the HMO market with an IPA plan of its own for another fifteen years. The only HMOs in the area were struggling, union-developed, prepaid group practice plans in the City of Philadelphia that would soon fold. The more desirable growing suburban market was ripe for picking.

Matching the price of traditional Blue Cross coverage was critical for the success of HMO/PA. The Philadelphia area had an oversupply of hospital beds and specialty physicians and this translated into much higher use of costly hospital care and high premiums for Blue Cross subscribers. It also strengthened the hand of HMO/PA in doing selective contracting with hospitals.

None of this would have mattered, had it not been for the 1973 federal HMO legislation that required employers to offer an HMO option if a federally qualified one was available in their region. This got HMO/PA's foot in the door of every employer in the Philadelphia region. All they had to do was a great selling job to the employees. They could offer coverage of preventive and primary care, in addition to the hospital coverage offered by the Blue Cross plan. They passed out apples, part of their trademark, at employee benefit meetings and promoted themselves as the plan that would keep people healthy. HMO/PA soon broke even and continued to grow.

In the 1980s, a profound shift took place in the federal HMO program and in the industry it was promoting (Gray, 2006). The Reagan Administration ended the federal grant program for the development of non-profit HMOs and the federal Office of Health Maintenance Organization assumed the new role of actively promoting HMOs as an opportunity for private investors. IPAs were the ideal vehicle for private investment, since they required little initial capital and offered the opportunity for rapid growth on a national scale. In addition, 1982 changes in the Medicare law permitted HMOs to receive 95% of the average age and sex adjusted per-capita Medicare fee for service cost in a county. In a high cost area like Philadelphia and similar metropolitan areas, this provided an additional potential opportunity for expansion.

Adding to the opportunities for HMO/PA, the Medicare program, followed by other health insurance plans, fundamentally changed the way hospitals were paid. The enactment of the Medicare Prospective Payment System (PPS) in 1983 shifted hospital payments to a flat rate per admission based on the average cost of their diagnostically related group (DRG). Hospital occupancy dropped precipitously as patient length of stay was reduced in order to increase profitability. The hospitals in most metropolitan areas now had excess capacity and were much more willing to cut deals for deeply discounted reimbursement with HMO/PA and other aggressive IPA plans. In exchange for the added volume of IPA admissions to take advantage of this excess capacity, they were willing to accept lower payments that would cover the additional cost and make a little contribution to their operating margin.

In addition, a long ignored provision of the federal Employee Retirement and Income Security Act of 1974 (ERISA) contributed immensely to the growth potential of IPAs. The intent of ERISA was to standardize corporate pension and benefit plans so that it would be easier for a multi-state corporate employer to offer a common benefit plan. If such companies "self-insured" and simply hired a third party administrator to collect premiums and pay claims, they were insulated from any state insurance regulatory oversight. IPAs, such as Abramson's, were set up to perform a third party administrator function. It was essentially what they were already doing, since a part of the risk in the plan had already been shifted onto providers through capitation payment arrangements.

Adding to the advantage of an astute player of the game such as Abramson, state regulation of conversion of non-profit plans to for-profits was lax and there was a lot of ambiguity about how assets of a non-profit plan should be valued in such a conversion. Leveraged buy-outs by managers of non-profit IPA plans could be done relatively easily with little regulatory or political resistance at what to many seemed a fraction of the real value of a plan (Gray, 2006).

None of these events escaped the attention of Len Abramson. HMO/PA was converted from a non-profit to a for-profit corporation in

December 1982. As part of this conversion process, Abramson repaid the federal grant he had received in creating HMO/PA. As a mark of his ambition for the HMO and the new opportunities he saw opening up, Abramson changed its name to U.S. Healthcare. The new U.S. Healthcare had 125,000 members at this point and was the fastest growing HMO in the nation. It could no longer be ignored by physicians in the Philadelphia area. In spite of its low payments and restrictive control over their practices, many felt they had no choice but to sign contracts. Although many of these U.S. Healthcare participating physicians seethed with resentment, most were silenced, fearing retaliation that would result in non-renewal of their contracts which would threaten the financial viability of their practices.

In 1983, U.S. Healthcare made an initial public offering of stock. The funds Abramson got from his stock offering allowed him to expand his HMO into new markets, first to New Jersey and then to the Midwest. He would face real HMO competition in some of these new markets, unlike the Philadelphia region. The Chicago area market was particularly competitive, but despite setbacks in Chicago, U.S. Healthcare continued to grow at a record clip, especially in Pennsylvania, New Jersey and a new Florida market. The all important goal for U.S. Healthcare became maximizing the number of members it served. A big HMO, it was believed, would have the greatest clout in negotiating low payments to physicians and hospitals and in keeping the costs to employers relatively low.

In 1985, U.S. Healthcare received federal permission to offer health services to Medicare recipients. It opened a trial in the Philadelphia area and became very selective at targeting only the counties with the highest average per capita costs that would assure profitability.

U.S. Healthcare emerged as the most profitable publicly traded HMO in the nation, with profits of $24.5 million in 1985. Since 1982, U.S. Healthcare had been growing an average of 85% a year. The bigger it grew, the more logical the U.S. Healthcare model seemed to be. Abramson emerged as a spokesperson for the HMO industry, speaking out against the sacred cows of American medicine such as the nation's teaching hospitals. Teaching hospitals traditionally argued that they were entitled to a higher level of reimbursement than their community hospital sisters because of the cost of their training programs. Abramson said insurance companies had an obligation to pay only for patient care. He argued that teaching costs should be covered by the endowments of teaching hospitals and by government subsidies. The more members U.S. Healthcare had, the less capacity teaching hospitals and other providers of care had to stand up to Abramson's HMO.

The next target of U.S. Healthcare was New York City, another highly competitive HMO market. U.S. Healthcare put a major marketing effort into New York and, within a year of beginning operations in 1985, had enrolled 200 physicians and 38 hospitals as participants. Despite stiff competition, the New York segment grew rapidly, accounting for 40% of U.S. Healthcare's revenues within five years.

As a result of these successes, Abramson came to view himself as something of a visionary. In 1990, he wrote a book called *Healing our Health Care System*, in which he contended that he had actually established a model for the future of healthcare in America.

"As the founder and chief executive of one of the nation's most successful health maintenance organization companies," he wrote, "I have been fortunate enough to prosper because I understand the healthcare industry. By applying American capitalism to healthcare, I have realized the American dream. I see this book as an opportunity for a partial payback. I am anxious to share my knowledge with you so that, together, we may help our country regain its rightful world leadership position in management, industry, economics and medicine" (Abramson, 1990).

The book included a scathing critique of non-profit hospitals, their billing practices and their lack of attention to the quality of care that patients receive. Noting that correctional facilities treat prisoners better than most hospitals treat sick people he observed that, "it is all too clear that the physician is the only customer of any concern to the hospital" (Abramson, 1990). His book received equally scathing reviews in the healthcare trade journals.

U.S. Healthcare in the 1990s continued to move to additional states and to maintain a high level of profitability. Its successes were watched with envy by Aetna, a large traditional indemnity insurance company that had struggled to break into the growing HMO market, convinced that growth and market share were the long term keys to profitability. In 1991, U.S. Healthcare reported earnings of $151 million on revenues of $1.7 billion. Enrollment growth and profitability continued over the next five years.

Aetna, with no awareness that the halcyon days of IPAs would soon end, turned its sights on the acquisition of U.S. Healthcare. Abramson, with the omniscience that marked his entire HMO career, knew the right time to get into the HMO business, and knew the right time to get out. In 1996, U.S. Healthcare was acquired by Aetna, Inc. at a cost of $8.3 billion. That amounted to $3,300 for every member of U.S. Healthcare, the highest price ever paid per covered enrollee in the industry's history. Abramson's equity in U.S. Healthcare made him a near billionaire at the time of the sale.

Discussion

- What opportunities did Leonard Abramson see in the healthcare insurance market in 1973 and how did he go about seizing them?
- Aetna made a careful and thorough assessment of its acquisition of U.S. Healthcare. The numbers and the forecasts of its potential contribution to their company all confirmed that the deal made sense. What did it miss?

Postscript

With eerily clockwork precision, the final unraveling of the HMO movement in the United States began with the Aetna acquisition of U.S. Healthcare in 1996.

In retrospect, the political support for HMOs had been buoyed by efforts to defeat the Clinton Administration healthcare reform proposal of 1993–94. Critics argued that the private sector was doing the job of controlling cost increases through fierce HMO market competition and the government should stay out of their way. Indeed, the rate of increase in health expenditures progressively declined between 1990 and 1996 (Catlin, Cowan *et al.*, 2007). While it coincided with the growth in market share of the HMO and the industry was quick to claim credit, it also followed a recession that made employers and public programs more willing to slash health benefits. The economic boom in the last half of the 1990s helped fuel a HMO backlash.

In 1996, the same year of the U.S. Healthcare acquisition, 1,000 pieces of legislation were introduced to state legislatures to further regulate or weaken HMOs and 53 laws were passed (Bodenheimer, 2006). Many physicians and consumers were angry and determined to curtail the control of HMOs. HMOs shifted from being the widely politically popular magic bullet to a target of abuse, particularly for their efforts to control use of specialty and hospital care.

> *An HMO member who had died arrived at heaven's gate. St. Peter asks the applicant if he belonged to an HMO and, getting an affirmative answer, denied the HMO participant admission saying: "you don't have prior approval."*

Such widely circulated jokes in 1996 ushered in the beginning of State legislative and regulatory reforms that would result in the abandonment of many of the practices that had helped propel the financial success of U.S. Healthcare.

The HMO share of the national health insurance market fell in the six years after 1997 from 32% to 26%. In the process, however, HMOs evolved into entities that were increasingly difficult to distinguish from traditional forms of health insurance coverage. Most of the remaining staff model HMOs became "mixed model" plans that included contracts with independent practitioners. IPAs dissolved into a complex array of products with varying degrees of restriction in choice of physician and hospital and prior approval of services. These products increasingly blurred the boundaries between the traditional health plan and HMOs.

The trade associations that represent organizations tell you much about who their members are and the common interests they share. The evolution of the trade associations representing health insurance plans tells the story of the demise of the HMO movement. In 1995, the American Association of Health Plans was formed from a merger of Group Health Association of America (previously representing the pre-paid group practices or staff model HMOs) and the American Managed Care and Review Association (which previously represented the IPAs). In the final burial of the HMO, in name if not in form, the American Association of Health Plans merged with the Health Insurance Institute of America (which represented traditional indemnity commercial health insurance plans) in 2003. The newly formed organization, called "America's Health Insurance Plans," describes itself on its website as "representing health insurance plans pro-viding medical, long-term care, disability income, dental, supplemental, stop loss and reinsurance to more than 200 million Americans" (America's Health Insurance Plans, 2009). There is no mention of pre-paid group practice, independent practice associations or HMOs in this description. The dream that drove the formation of pre-paid group prac-tice plans, of providing physicians with a protective environment where their decisions about treatment would be insulated from concerns about how their patients would pay for it, is, for the most part, dead.

In acquiring U.S. Healthcare, as the above suggests, Aetna made a bad decision and had even worse timing (Robinson, 2004). The merged Aetna-U.S. Healthcare initially looked largely to the historical U.S. Healthcare's IPA model and growth strategy just as market momentum was shifting away from such a model. Overall, Aetna-U.S. Healthcare plan enrollment peaked in 1999 and then declined, as did profit margins which fell to 1.65% in 2001. Its stock price, which had peaked at $82 in 1997, the year after the acquisition, plunged to $25 a share in early 2001. Under pressure from the board, the entire executive leadership, including those who came to it from U.S. Healthcare's management ranks, left the company. Abramson, who had served on its board, also resigned. The subsequent re-structuring produced a more diversified line of insurance and third party administrator products focused on the more profitable segments of the market. U.S. Healthcare was dropped from the name of the company and is no longer mentioned (Robinson, 2004). Aetna Inc.'s restructuring mir-rored that of the health insurance industry as a whole, marking an end to U.S. Healthcare and the HMO era in which it had flourished.

Abramson, in retirement from U.S. Healthcare, has transformed, himself into a philanthropist, making major contributions to academic health center research programs and service providers in the region. He serves as a trustee of Johns Hopkins University, The Children's Hospital of Philadelphia and the Brookings Institution and splits his time between a family compound outside Philadelphia and an estate in Jupiter, Florida.

In the Philadelphia market, Independence Blue Cross (IBC), the Philadelphia area's Blue Cross plan, has regained its dominant position after surviving the fierce head-to-head competition with U.S. Healthcare in the 1990s. Ironically, their long history as a traditional insurance plan made them the major enrollment beneficiary of the HMO backlash in the region. Similar to other for-profit and non-profit plans, IBC now offers a bewildering array of products to employers, essentially tailoring them individually in terms of premiums and benefits. More choice of providers and more benefits meant higher premiums. More restrictive choices and more limited benefits meant lower premiums. The administrative difficulties of managing such an array of individually tailored products is simplified by using the same network of providers for all of them, which also increases the stakes for providers in successfully negotiating a contract with IBC. A heavy investment by IBC in a web-based electronic claims processing system for their provider network essentially eliminates the administrative burden of such individually tailored plans for IBC, its network of physicians and individuals covered by such benefits.

IBC has tried to soft-pedal utilization controls and has invested heavily in disease management programs, employing more nurses than most of the hospitals it contracts with. It has done this partly in hopes of improving the quality of care for those with one of the twenty-two most common and costly chronic conditions. It has also done it in the hope that it will reduce costs and help the negative image resulting from physicians unhappy about increasingly restrictive payment contracts and consumers unhappy about restrictions on the care they can receive.

Just as in other health plans, growth is assumed to be essential for long term survival. A merger of IBC with the Pittsburgh area Blue Cross Plan, WellPoint that had been brewing for several years, was called off by the two parties at the last minute in January 2009. The merged plan would have created one of the largest plans in the country and, some believe, would have eventually led to a for-profit conversion. The merger negotiations involved billions of dollars in assets and complex, lengthy and costly negotiations. In a last minute attempt to assure a modicum of competition in the Pennsylvania health insurance market, the Pennsylvania Insurance Commissioner insisted that they give up one of their trademark names, Blue Cross or Blue Shield. This sticking point effectively ended the merger negotiations. The Commissioner had argued that dropping one of the trademark names would allow for competition from another Blue Cross or Blue Shield plan. But what is so powerful about such a name? These were

names, created in the 1930s, as part of an effort of local providers to create a voluntary self-help program to assure that everyone that needed hospital or medical care could receive it. These efforts were shaped by the
earlier sickness funds of lodges and fraternal orders that made members
responsible for caring for each other. Should the name of this vestigial
organ from our past have any value at all? Yet, no commercial plan or
health maintenance organization has ever been successful at developing
a trademark that comes close to resonating so well with the American
public. Indeed, the frantic era of for-profit HMO development that
Len Abramson rode out with such success did much to increase its value.

Discussion

- Were the two Blues in Pennsylvania correct in abandoning their
  merger over this condition?
- A universal national health insurance program would probably use
  many of the same strategies to control costs that HMOs have used.
  Could this be more successful? If so, how?

Case 8: The Office of Medical Assistance
and HealthChoices

Background

Just as HMOs in the private sector were beginning their decline into obliv-
ion, public sector ones, Medicaid HMOs, were rising from these ashes.
Financing medical care for the medically indigent has always operated on a
different track, being part of a tiered system of care. County and municipal
governments assumed the bulk of the financial responsibility for this care
up into the 1950s. County, municipal and voluntary clinics and hospitals,
assisted by medical teaching programs, provided the indigent care. State
governments provided some subsidies for these efforts. As early as the
1890s, the Pennsylvania legislature provided a special fixed amount appropriation to some of the voluntary hospitals in Philadelphia to support indigent care. Just like the lodge practices to private HMOs, this was the early
precursor to Medicaid HMO per capita payments. Medical schools have

always relied on a large indigent population for teaching purposes. In the heady days after the passage of Medicare and Medicaid, it appeared possible the tiered structure of care would end, and there was rising concern among medical schools about the loss of teaching material to private practice. The low Medicaid payments to physicians for office visits, however, assured a low participation rate of private doctors in most urban areas where medical schools were located and this soon alleviated their concerns.

Rising costs in the Medicaid program produced a long string of efforts to bring them under control. These efforts faced two seemingly intractable problems: (1) curtailing costs without further imperiling the health of a vulnerable and dependent population and (2) avoiding the cream-skimming risk selection problem of HMOs that stalled cost-saving efforts in the private sector.

There would seem to be an easy way to cut costs in a healthcare plan — just raise the cost sharing by the beneficiary. If they pay more upfront in terms of a deductible and higher coinsurance, not only will some of the cost be shifted onto them, they will be more frugal users of services and the total cost should be less. This begged the question, how would the increased cost sharing affect the quality of care received and their health? Federal policy makers conducted a national experiment to attempt to answer this question, the Rand Health Insurance Experiment. It was a massive, multimillion dollar randomized clinical trial involving some 7,700 subjects. Conducted between 1971 and 1982, it randomly assigned families to different "treatments" in terms of cost sharing and measured the effects. This is the only rigorous experimental study on this question ever conducted — no similar study will probably ever be done again because of increased human subject approval requirements.[9] In essence, the conclusion of the study, which compared no cost sharing, 25%, 50% or 95%

_____

[9] In 1972, a year after the implementation of the Rand Health Insurance Experiment, press reports on the Public Health Service Tuskegee Syphilis Study, where black patients with syphilis were assigned to an untreated control group so that the effects could be observed even after definitive treatment become available. This produced a political firestorm. It led to requiring an Internal Review Board approval for any study involving human subjects and much tighter subject protections. A Rand type study, withdrawing treatment by raising the financial barriers to care for some subjects, probably would not be approved in the current environment.

coinsurance and those assigned to a pre-paid group practice. The two basic conclusions were: (1) yes, cost sharing reduces use and cost but it also causes delays in seeking care and some reduction in needed care and (2) *except for poorer or sicker participants,* cost sharing appears to have had little effect on health (Rand Corporation, 2008). The lodges and fraternal orders one hundred years earlier had come to similar conclusions in meeting the needs of their members. For state Medicaid programs responsible for the poorer and sicker who could not afford even limited cost sharing, these conclusions did not help.

Medicaid programs began to experiment with providing their beneficiaries options to join HMOs. These early experiments were not encouraging. A fee-for-service system billing process tracks what services providers are billing for. A Medicaid HMO gets a monthly payment based on the number of Medicaid enrollees in their plan or at least the number who they say are their enrollees. How do you make sure they are actually providing appropriate services for their premium payments? There were plenty of horror stories in California and Florida about fly-by-night HMOs that grabbed Medicaid recipients outside the welfare office and got them to enroll in exchange for a package of free diapers or a gift certificate for a free meal at a fast food restaurant. The provider networks of these plans were limited or non-existent and the Medicaid recipients had to resort to getting their care in hospital emergency rooms. More careful selection of plans and more rigorous policing could eliminate most of these problems. The more intractable problem was the same problem that employers faced with providing HMO options to their employees — cream-skimming risk selection. The HMOs that would get perhaps 80% or 90% of the average cost per Medicaid recipient as a monthly premium would selectively enroll those so that the average cost would be only 50% of the premium payment and pocket the windfall profits. The costs of those who remained in the traditional Medicaid fee-for-service system would skyrocket.

In 1996, coinciding with the purchase of U.S. Healthcare by Aetna and the beginning of the HMO backlash and stagnated overall growth in HMO enrollment, the Medicaid HMO enrollment began to take off. Learning from their previous HMO experience, state Medicaid programs began to engineer a transformation that radically changed not just the Medicaid system but had a profound impact on the health system as a whole.

Nowhere was fee-for-service more irrational than in the state Medicaid programs. In order to save money, fees to doctors were fixed at levels well below reasonable cost. Unlike doctors who could opt out of the Medicaid program if they did not like what they were being offered, hospitals could not. It accounted for too large a portion of their income, they could not relocate as easily and they were required by law to provide medically essential care anyway. As a result, hospitals and their state associations bargained hard with the state Medicaid programs and got paid something much closer to actual cost for inpatient care. Predictably, Medicaid patients had trouble getting basic primary and preventive care, but much less trouble being admitted for a costly hospital stay.

The outpatient and hospital care was costly, lousy care and no provider, consumer or state purchaser liked it. It seemed to invite abuse. It was also a headache from the state Medicaid program's perspective since it was impossible to budget and predict costs. As a result, state Medicaid programs would often run out of money before the end of the fiscal year, hold up payments to providers and try to get a special appropriation through the legislature to cover the shortfall. This did not win many friends in the provider community or in the state legislature.

What the Pennsylvania Medicaid program wanted to do, was make market competition and choice work for their Medicaid recipients. It was a brilliant political strategy. To be against choice and market competition seemed un-American. Indeed, medical associations had waged a successful campaign against the Truman National Health Insurance plan, arguing that "compulsory" health insurance was the first step towards communist enslavement and had raised similar concerns over the passage of Medicare. The new plan for Pennsylvania's Medicaid program embraced choice and market competition while addressing the cream-skimming risk selection problem that troubled the private employer and Medicare HMO competitive market free choice initiatives.

What Pennsylvania's Medicaid program developed was an ingenious approach, using the lessons learned from earlier state Medicaid managed care experiments. It became one of a few state models soon adopted in some form by most other state medical assistance programs. The Philadelphia region became the testing ground for this model in 1997 and it turned its healthcare system upside down.

The HealthChoices Model

From the point of view of key staff in the Pennsylvania Medical Assistance Program, there were three main problems that needed to be addressed in the re-design of the program.

1. *Poor access to good primary and preventive services:* Most private practicing physicians, particularly in areas with a high concentration of Medicaid patients (e.g. urban inner city), either did not accept any Medicaid patients or did not accept new ones. This left the provision of much of the preventive and primary care Medicaid beneficiaries got, to emergency rooms, the city health centers of limited capacity, and substandard Medicaid mills.

2. *Irrational incentives:* Physicians got fee-for-service with fees well below reasonable cost. The only way to make money on a predominantly Medicaid practice was to generate lots of services per visit turning the practice into what was derisively described as a "Medicaid mill." The typical Medicaid mill visit would involve the provision of many billable services. Patients were "ping ponged" back and forth getting diagnostic tests, X-rays, physical therapy, podiatric consultations, etc. Many of these services were unnecessary and, in some of the worst practices, showed up on the bills and were not even performed at all. The incentives for hospitals were even worse. They could lose money caring for a person in the emergency room or hospital clinic or admit them as an inpatient and get a reasonable contribution to their operating margin. Hospital days per 1,000 Medicaid recipients were two to three times the days per thousand for private pay recipients. There was little incentive to provide routine preventive care that might prevent emergency room use and inpatient admissions in the first place.

3. *No budgetary predictability:* The Medicaid program costs were a function of the number of beneficiaries and the number of services they would receive. It was hard to predict the number of services and this often resulted in budgetary shortfalls. This would result in long delays in paying providers and lots of frustration and finger pointing.

In short, the state Medicaid program cost a lot of money to produce poor results. In fiscal year 1996, the total cost of the program was

$6.2 billion dollars, there were 1.6 million recipients and the average cost of coverage per recipient was $3,634. It provided limited access to primary care and excessive use of both emergency departments and inpatient hospital care. Care was fragmented and often of poor quality.

The HealthChoices programmatically redesigned the Medicaid program for the Philadelphia Metropolitan Area to: (1) assure better access to primary and preventive services, (2) control cost increases and (3) make the budgetary commitments predictable. In spite of the hand wringing on the part of service providers and welfare advocates, it largely achieved these objectives (Hurley, Zinn *et al.*, 1999).

The HealthChoices Plan, which initially encompassed all Medicaid beneficiaries in the five county Philadelphia Metropolitan Area, included three core elements:

1. *Regional Global Capitation*: In 1996, in the five county metropolitan area of Philadelphia, the Medicaid program had expended a total $2.7 billion on Medicaid beneficiaries. Dividing this figure by the number of Medicaid beneficiaries that year produced the per capita cost. The state offered 85% of this per capita cost as the basis for calculating premium payments to health plans enrolling Medicaid beneficiaries. Actual premiums for the plans were adjusted for inflation and case mix.
2. *Full Risk Contracting with Plans*: Each plan agreed to assume risk and provide a basic benefit package for this premium. They had to use a portion of the premium to contract with primary care physicians and a portion of this premium as a pool of funds to cover the cost of specialty referrals and inpatient hospital care. Since some previous plans had become insolvent, leaving providers unpaid and beneficiaries uncared for, plans were required to meet equity, re-insurance, and insolvency requirements to assure payments to providers. It also imposed a number of reporting requirements on plans to try to reduce the risk of abuse and substandard care.
3. *Competition*: Medicaid recipients could "choose" one of the competing plans. While those choices were partly illusory, they helped sell the program as a competitive, market-oriented solution. Indeed, HealthChoices actually restricted the choices of recipients compared to the traditional fee-for-service model. The primary care physician

also restricted choice by serving as the "gatekeeper" for specialty services and hospitalizations, receiving a share of the savings for reducing expenditures for these services. Also, the health plans could selectively choose to contract with only some physicians and hospitals. Choice had produced abuses in previous Medicaid managed care programs. HealthChoices prohibited plans from enrolling members or directly marketing to them. They sub-contracted with a separate organization to enroll beneficiaries and explain their options.

Results

What happened? It should not come as a surprise that the state got what it wanted in budget predictability and savings. HealthChoices was designed to provide that predictability and to take the savings up front. What was more of an open question was whether providers would agree to participate in the program. Many primary care physicians and specialists had chosen not to participate in the traditional fee-for-service Medical Assistance program. At least initially, the primary care access problems largely disappeared in the HealthChoices program. Freed of the burden of extracting payment from the Medicaid program that physicians claimed cost more to manage than the payments they received and assured a guaranteed monthly flow of dollars in terms of their share of the premiums, private primary care practices opened their doors. Teaching hospitals that had long regarded the Medicaid clinics they provided as a reluctant burden ran the numbers and realized that they could not afford to lose these patients. If these patients flowed to their competitors, their financial viability would be threatened. The shabby benches in poorly lit corridors disappeared. Teaching hospitals hired their own primary care physicians, renovated their clinics, and constructed satellite offices providing more attractive surroundings for medical assistance patients than what typically existed in most private suburban practices. The primary care practices now had an incentive to actively manage the care of their clients and produced a modest reduction in the use of emergency rooms and an improvement in preventive care. It was not perfect, but it was more rational than what existed before. A little thought in how to design a way to best allocate the gold — in this case, about $3 billion dollars — goes a long way. Gold rules.

Discussion

- Changing the financial incentives changes the potential problems. While shifting the risk onto health plans and providers eliminates unnecessary incentives, it creates an incentive to forego providing services that are necessary. What safeguards are built into HealthChoices to prevent this from happening? What additional ones might be worth considering?

- National health insurance plans in other countries follow a model similar to HealthChoices. They develop a regional budget and allocate these resources to providers accordingly, either through health plans or directly. Suppose one were to combine the dollars flowing to private insurance carriers and Medicare into the HealthChoices program creating a single global regional capitation premium that health plans would contract with. What advantages and disadvantages would this have?

Postscript

The model that began in 1997 in the five county area of Philadelphia now covers 22 counties, approximately half of the Medicaid beneficiaries in the state and 46% of the Medicaid payments (Lewin Group, 2006, page 3). No one is arguing for a return to the old fee-for-service system. A comparative evaluation by the Lewin Group of HealthChoices and the fee-for-service program in Pennsylvania found that the average annual cost escalation in the HealthChoices areas was 7.4%, compared to 10.4% in the fee-for-service areas in the state, saving more than $2.7 billion. The HealthChoices plan also performed better in improving access to beneficiaries, quality of care and integration of services. Furthermore, it has become a model for other states and the Lewin Group estimates that full conversion to such a model could achieve overall savings of as much as $83 billion over a ten year period without the adverse effect of the alternative cost cutting strategies of limiting eligibility, eliminating covered benefits or reducing payment to providers. In addition the HealthChoices model, arguably, improved access and the quality of care to Medicaid patients.

The problem comes when the state Medicaid program, facing increased fiscal pressures, squeezes too hard in controlling cost increases, producing an adverse domino effect. Fewer plans are willing to negotiate contracts and those that do are Medical Assistance only plans. The hope of creating a single mainstream health plan system no longer exists. One plan in the Philadelphia area now controls 60% of the market and in some of the suburban counties, it has a virtual monopoly, eliminating any possibility of choice. The plans, squeezed by state premiums, have to squeeze providers and some providers have dropped out. Access to obstetricians is particularly a problem for HealthChoices recipients and some hospitals have refused to sign contracts with some of the plans. Perhaps one saving grace is that the two largest HealthChoices plans are local organizations partly owned by hospital providers (Health Partners of Philadelphia and Keystone Mercy Health Plan). They are the only remaining plans with some provider ownership in the Philadelphia market. If the financial pressures get too great, these plans could be sold to national firms and the local provider flavor and service driven mission of these plans could be lost.

One of the arguments in the Lewin Group assessment of the usefulness of the HealthChoices model is its ability to insulate the Medicaid program from the pressures of powerful provider groups to increase payments in the fee-for-service system. HealthChoices, however, faces political pressure groups as well, but different ones. In 2008, the governor proposed centralizing drug purchasing for the Medicaid program in the Department of Public Welfare that would make possible savings of $95 million a year. This proposal was blocked by Republicans in the legislature with the support of powerful managed care and drug-company lobbies (Goldstein, 2008). When there is enough money at stake, there will always be political pressure on health plans, whether public or private.

Discussion

- How does local provider ownership affect the decisions of a Medicaid managed care plan? How would a shift to a national commercial insurance company ownership change this? Would it make any difference?
- In the 19th century, some of the non-profit hospitals in Philadelphia received a direct appropriation from the state legislature to help take care of the poor. How do the HealthChoices health plan payments to hospitals differ from this?

6

The Market:
Why It Doesn't Work — Or Does It?

Working the Market

Do competitive markets make healthcare better? The problem is that the game does not end with how health plans design the field of play. Providers adapt and the way they adapt does not always work to the benefit of health plans or their subscribers. For providers, it boils down to two numbers multiplied together: price and volume. The product of these two numbers determines how much money a hospital or physician practice takes in. The more volume increases, the lower the cost per unit. Some costs, such as debt services, are fixed, meaning they do not change with volume. These costs just get spread over more units. Usually, the more volume, the more efficient you get so the variable cost per unit may decline as well. In theory, in competitive healthcare markets, lower prices and better services attract higher volume and the consumer wins — or do they?

Markets, like the jungle, work in a primitive way — everyone is a predator. If prices are high relative to the costs, more providers will enter the market and the volume of patients seen by individual providers will decline. Health plans, as a result, can then prey on providers by doing selective contracting, exchanging larger volume for discounted prices, and weeding out the oversupply. Providers can defend against this by also becoming predators, seeking out the easiest prey by being more selective about the patients they take, carving out niches, and specializing in the most profitable procedures. The real world outcome of all this is more fragmented, costly and, on the whole, poorer quality healthcare. The problem is that perfect markets, at least in the provision of healthcare, have never existed and never will because we do not like the consequences.

In this chapter we will look at three cases. Case 9 deals with the efforts of primary care doctors to escape the rat race of high volume practice. Case 10 deals with an example of the focused factory approach, carving out a specialized line and its impact on the rest of the health system. Case 11 deals with the special case of heart transplants and the effort to find a more appropriate way to allocate scarce and precious resources. In each of these cases, is a market driven approach guilty of producing poorer quality, higher costs and greater human suffering? The jury is still out.

Case 9: Concierge Medicine

Background

> *"Are you working harder for the same money? Doctors' pay is falling and primary care doctors who are already among the lowest paid physicians have faced the steepest decline in earnings. We can help you run your practice the way you've dreamed, spending the time you need with each patient, researching each case to provide the best treatment, having the time to counsel patients in a way that enhances patient compliance yielding great outcomes and, most importantly, freeing you of the financial concerns imposed by declining reimbursement."*
>
> *(MDVIP, 2008)*

Indeed, what doctor would not want to practice like this and what patient would not want to be cared for in such a practice? This is the pitch of MDVIP, the largest packager of a rapidly growing new form of primary care, known as Concierge Medicine. For an extra fee, the growing hassles for the patient and physician disappear.

For a brief period in the early 1990s, a lot of primary care doctors felt they were finally beginning to reap the financial rewards, respect and influence they deserved. They were the centerpiece, the gatekeepers of the managed care system and were now the ones calling the shots rather than the hospital specialists. They were paid for providing this critical gatekeeper role. Managed care plans in most areas were competing for their business and, for new primary care physicians, they were in a sellers' market. Then everything started to look less rosy. Payments shrank and many practices had to carry higher patient loads or face a decline in income. Managed care plans started demanding more, which meant more paperwork and more difficulties in getting patients the specialty and diagnostic care they needed. In response to these changes, the number of new medical graduates choosing to go into primary care declined and there appeared to be a growing shortage of primary care physicians. Patients noticed the changes and were not happy about them. Busier practices produced more mistakes, more unhappy patients, and higher malpractice risks. MDVIP offered a simple prescription for all of these problems.

The MDVIP Prescription

The pitch made by MDVIP to primary care physicians went something like this. Work with us and convert your 3,000 patient practice with as many as 30 visits a day to a 600 patient practice with about 4–6 patient visits a day. Instead of brief and hectic visits that last five to ten minutes after long waits, you can provide same day appointments that start on time and last an hour. We'll help you supplement what you get from Medicare and private insurance carriers with a $1,650 annual private retainer fee. The $990,000 (a 600 patient practice times the $1,650 retainer fee) in private retainer fees will more than offset the decline in insurance payments from your larger volume practice. (Some concierge style practices charge as much as $20,000 a year, limit themselves to even fewer patients and a few refuse to take any insurance payments). For less than what people spend per month on cigarettes and unhealthy snacks, MDVIP argues, you can provide them with an easily affordable, convenient package of services that will assure their optimal health. MDVIP will provide you with the guidance and support needed to make the transition to this form of practice successful. Practices that work with us get a package of services (an individual website for each patient, a wellness plan, an electronic medical record they can keep with them and an array of office practice services) that add value for your patient and assist you in providing state-of-the-art personalized care. Our growing network of physicians gives your practice high quality brand name recognition and we can assist in overcoming the insurance and regulatory hurdles associated with this new form of practice (MDVIP, 2008). What MDVIP doctors offer to their patients in return for their retainer fee is 24-hour availability, same or next day appointments, a comprehensive physical, a package of personal wellness and prevention services, and assistance in coordinating specialist appointments at premier medical institutions.

MDVIP as a Business

MDVIP has grown rapidly from its base in Boca Raton, Florida and now has 280 affiliated physicians located in 26 states and the District of Columbia serving more than 95,000 patients (MDVIP, 2008). For the services it provides practices, MDVIP takes a cut from the retainer fee of members of about $500, generating approximately $47.5 million in revenues for the company (Zuger, 2005). MDVIP selects practices for its network located in well insured, affluent areas and with patients with similar characteristics. They seek well trained, motivated primary care physicians with good interpersonal skills who are willing to work with them in enhancing the services they provide to patients. The patient population and physician characteristics help ensure a successful transition. MDVIP provides assistance in transitioning and marketing the new practice, state and federal regulatory guidance, call-center services, insurance plan billing support, electronic medical records, staff training, quality control reviews and the billing and collection of the retainer fees. A privately held venture, it received $6 million from Summit Partners in 2005, a private equity/venture capital firm (Stolz, 2007).

MDVIP has proved adept at overcoming some of the state and federal insurance regulatory barriers experienced by concierge practices. Their physicians receive Medicare payments for many of their patients. Medicare prohibits physicians from balance billing or asking patients to pay the difference between the fees Medicare will pay and what the physician wants for the same service. It is also illegal to double-bill for the same service. In 2002, after a letter to the Secretary of the Department of Health and Human Services (DHHS) from five senators expressed concern over the legality of concierge Medicare billing practices, DHHS conducted a formal review. Tommy Thompson, who served as Secretary of DHHS at that time, concluded that, as long as the retainer fee was clearly for services not covered by Medicare, collecting such retainer fees did not violate the law (Zuger, 2005). However, that left unresolved exactly what services are clearly not covered. MDVIP has been careful to emphasize the additional preventive and wellness services that its practices offer which are not covered by Medicare. It also soft-pedals the "queue jumping" advantages that would make the additional retainer fees more questionable. Indeed, shortly after stepping down as Secretary of DHHS, Thompson received a retainer of his own from MDVIP. In July 2005, MDVIP created the Committee on Cost Reduction through Preventive Care, chaired by former Secretary of Health and Human Services Tommy G. Thompson. "MDVIP is currently working with Secretary Thompson to improve the lives of patients as well as the economics of this nation's healthcare system" (MDVIP, 2008). According to press accounts, MDVIP is evidently one of "a vast portfolio of private sector pursuits, many of them in healthcare" that the former Secretary has taken on since stepping down (Skiba, 2006).

Discussion

- A young physician friend has asked your advice about joining MDVIP. Based on the information provided, what would you tell him/her?
- What kind of long term impact would you expect that the expansion of such retainer practices will have on the organization of healthcare in the United States?

Postscript

Simple, attractive solutions to healthcare problems are never as simple or as attractive as they first appear.

One of the basic rules of health insurance is that the "price sets the experience." That is, if a person chooses to pay for a supplemental health insurance plan, the chances are that they will make use of it. One could argue that MDVIP physicians are essentially providing a supplemental insurance plan and there will be adverse risk selection into that plan. People who want or need more services will be the ones most likely to pay the extra $1,650 out of their pockets. A MDVIP practice may cut the number of patients by 80%, but the number of patient contacts, the time involved and the level of effort involved will not drop that much. There are bits and pieces of anecdotal evidence suggesting that things are playing out this way with the worried well, hypochondriacs, and those with multiple complex chronic conditions over-represented in concierge style practices. A primary care physician in Massachusetts who had spent $100,000 in consultant and marketing fees to set up a concierge practice discovered that more than half of the patients that signed up were over the age of seventy-five. Many demanded house calls. "They'd call me on weekends, telling me that they were feeling better" (Zipkin, 2005). Disappointed with concierge style practice, he closed down the practice and works in an emergency room of a local hospital where he feels he has greater control over his life. The expectation of some concierge practice patients seems to be, "I paid for you and I own you." Physicians do not like being treated like domestic servants. Indeed, physicians involved in these practices now do not even mention the word concierge in the description of their form of practice. The major association involved in representing such practices now calls itself "The Society for Innovative Medical Practice Design."

A few concierge practices refuse any contracts with insurance plans and just take payments directly from their patients. These practices face no problems.

However, the vast majority of these practices, just like MDVIP's, want to have their cake and eat it too. They get payments for their services from health plans and rely on the retainer fee to help supplement these payments. This is a potential problem. The federal Medicare duplicate and balance billing issues were left unresolved by Secretary Thompson's brief and superficial dismissal. Concierge physicians choosing to continue to participate in the Medicare program may continue to face difficulty clearly asserting that they are not charging for services for which they have already been paid by Medicare. They could be held liable under the False Claims Act for penalties of $5,000 – $10,000, plus three times the damages sustained by the government. It is difficult to clearly distinguish between covered and uncovered services. For example, Medicare has recently begun to cover preventive services and periodic physical examinations, overlapping what MDVIP practices claim to provide as a supplemental service. In another example, a physician was fined for double-billing patients because he charged a $600 annual fee for "coordination of care, a comprehensive assessment and plan for optimum health, and extra time spent on patient care" (Rose, 2004).

Charging a flat annual fee, as MDVIP does, also opens up another potential Pandora's Box. Are the MDVIP physicians selling an unlicensed insurance product? State insurance departments are responsible for protecting consumers through the licensing or registration of insurance products, assuring adequate reserves, an acceptable history of past business practices, etc. Assuming that such practices had to be licensed as insurance products, some of these requirements would present costly and difficult hurdles.

In addition, managed care plans that *are* licensed by the state and contract with physicians to be a part of their network of providers may also have problems with the MDVIP retainer fee arrangements. (Managed care plans also offer Medicare Advantage products that provide an alternative to the traditional plan for Medicare patients.) Most of these plans have "hold harmless" provisions in their contracts with physicians that prohibit them from seeking additional payments from patients covered by the plan. Since all health plan network physicians must also provide assurance of reasonable access, MDVIP arrangements for assuring access could be interpreted as falling under the hold harmless provisions. In addition, the state insurance departments also require that the plans, through their network physicians, assure non-discriminatory access for all their enrollees. The state insurance commissioners in New York and New Jersey have informed their plans that physicians charging access fees should not participate in their networks (Carnahan, 2006). In New Jersey, the insurance commissioner has gone further, concluding that this should apply even if the access fee is limited to services not covered by the health plan. Concerned about these issues, the Harvard Pilgrim Health Plan in Massachusetts has chosen not to accept physicians charging access fees into its network, which includes more than 21,000 physicians (Carnahan, 2006).

There is also a more troubling underlying question about concierge practices. Their real selling point from the perspective of most consumers and certainly highlighted in MDVIP's promotional materials is not convenience, but rather a higher quality of care. Patients pay the fee because they expect to receive prompter, more thorough and, as a consequence, higher quality care. That means a higher chance that potentially life threatening conditions will be diagnosed and appropriately treated early enough so that death and disability can be prevented. Does this mean that such practices, with the implicit assurances provided in exchange for the retainer fee, will be held to a higher standard in terms of malpractice? If that interpretation were taken by the courts, as it already is by those advocating or choosing to be cared for in such practices, it would not only alter malpractice risks, it would profoundly alter the role of the medical profession in the social fabric of our society.

There is an "easy" way to fix this in terms of laws and regulation, but it would certainly create new problems. One could impose limits on the size of all practices contracting with Medicare and other health plans, as has been imposed on the hours worked by hospital residents. This would probably increase access problems, given the growing shortage of primary care physicians. State or federal legislation or regulation could also either restrict or prohibit physicians from receiving additional payments if they have already been contracted to receive payments from a health plan. Such legislation and regulations have not been seriously considered until now, because concierge medicine was perceived to be a "self-limiting problem." That is, it is assumed that there are only so many people who are willing and can afford these additional payments and not enough to affect access to care for the rest of the insured population. The Government Accountability Office (GAO), in a review of its impact on beneficiary's access to Medicare, concluded that "overall access to physician services suggests that concierge care does not present a systematic problem at this time" (Government Accountability Office, 2005). DHHS indicated it agreed with these findings and will continue to monitor developments. At the time the GAO report came out in 2005, MDVIP, the largest retainer care network, had a total of 85 physicians serving 27,000 patients. In 2008, MDVIP reported a network of 280 physicians serving 95,000 patients, a more than threefold growth in less than three years. Nothing in these numbers or in MDVIP's assessments of its own growth opportunities would suggest that concierge practice is self-limiting.

Since concierge medicine cannot be dismissed anymore as an insignificant anomaly that has no impact on access to the insured population as a whole, it forces us to address the policy and the ethical questions this form of medical practice raises. Are patients that have become dependent on the care of a physician making a choice for this new form of care or does it represent a form of extortion? Faced with a shrinking supply of primary care practice options, are patients being abandoned by physicians who transition to this form of practice? These and related questions about medical ethics, of course, cannot be answered without addressing the broader questions about what kind of a health system we are creating and what kind of a society will be the result.

Discussion

- At the same time concierge practice has been developing, another challenge to primary care practice has emerged. Retail chains such as Wal-Mart, CVS and Walgreen's are creating walk-in clinics in their stores staffed mostly with nurse practitioners. They can handle a substantial portion of what takes place in a primary care physician's office. The combination of the expansion of concierge practice, retail practice and the decline in interest of medical graduates in primary care practice careers may doom the traditional forms of primary care practice to extinction. Would this represent progress or the further erosion of the status of physicians and of a single standard of care? What should be done either to prevent this from happening, or ensure that all benefit from this transformation?
- Simply ensuring that everyone is covered by health insurance, does not ensure that everyone has access to care. If too many primary care physicians choose to enter a concierge type practice, this new barrier to access will just replace the old insurance ones. What is the best way to prevent this from happening?

Case 10: Barix Clinics: The Case of the Focused Fat Factory

Background

"I skate to where the puck is going to be," hockey star Wayne Gretzky once explained. That quotation has often been used as the mantra of many entrepreneurs creating new business ventures. Barix Clinics, jumping on three converging trends, certainly seemed to be skating to the right place. The three trends included: (1) increasing obesity rates, (2) a looming bare-knuckle battle between general acute hospitals and hospital specialists over shrinking reimbursement dollars, and (3) the aggressive promotion of "consumer driven focused factory" solutions to the health system's problems.

More than one third of U.S. adults — more than 72 million — are obese. The prevalence of obesity has more than doubled for adults and tripled for children since 1980 (Flegal, Carroll *et al.*, 1998; Center for Disease Control, 2009). Obesity dramatically increases rates of coronary heart disease, type 2 diabetes, cancer, hypertension, stroke, osteoarthritis and many other chronic conditions in a population. The cost of obesity related healthcare in 2000 was estimated at $117 billion and since 1987, it has accounted for about 27% of the increases in medical costs (Center for Disease Control, 2009). The long advocated remedies of diet and exercise have proved ineffective at curbing the increase in obesity. For the morbidly obese — those roughly more than 100 pounds overweight and facing life threatening related medical conditions — bariatric surgery may be the best option. Bariatric surgery, which involves modification of the gastrointestinal tract to reduce nutrient intake or absorption, has produced dramatic weight loss and improved health for some patients. The number of such procedures has increased dramatically, quadrupling between 1998 and 2002. Patient outcomes have improved and death rates declined (Encinosa, Bernard *et al.*, 2005). It is not, however, a magic bullet. Serious complications and even death can result. About 40% of patients having the procedure develop a complication within 6 months (Agency for Healthcare Research and Quality, 2006). Complication rates differ by facility and surgeon and tend to improve with experience and as the number of procedures increase (Encinosa, Bernard *et al.*, 2005).

As both hospital specialists and general hospitals struggle over shrinking reimbursement from health plans, both have sought to capture a larger share of these dollars. Specialty hospitals, owned in part by the hospital specialists who practice in them, have been one way for hospital specialist physicians to do this. A GAO study identified more than 100 such specialty facilities and found that the number of specialty hospitals had tripled since 1990. About 70% had physician ownership and, of this 70%, half were totally owned by physicians (Government Accountability Office, 2003). The most common specialty hospitals focus on performing cardiac, orthopedic or other surgical procedures. They have, however, become the focus of an ongoing and contentious debate both at the federal policy level and within local medical communities.

A federal law, known as the Stark Anti-referral Law, prohibits physicians from referring Medicare patients to facilities in which they have a financial interest. A loophole in the law, however, permits physician ownership of an entire hospital rather than a specialized service. A moratorium was put in place by Congress in 2004 preventing Medicare from entering into any new contracts with specialty hospitals for services until the Stark-related implications could be more carefully assessed. Most health insurers follow in the wake of the federal government's massive Medicare program, so whatever policy decisions concerning Medicare payment are made tend to have a ripple effect in the rest of the health insurance market and are followed closely by everyone in the health sector. While the moratorium was eventually lifted, a fierce debate over the role and appropriateness of such facilities continues.

Opponents of physician-owned specialty hospitals argue that they skim the cream, siphoning off the more profitable business, caring for the well insured, but failing to provide the more costly essential services that ensure the safety of patients. The lack of emergency services has long been a particular concern of critics such as Senators Grassley (R-Iowa) and Baucus (D-Mont). They called attention to two deaths that took place in specialty hospitals without emergency services. One was from respiratory arrest following elective spinal fusion in Abilene, Texas and the other was from a heart attack after elective back surgery in Portland, Oregon. In both cases, the staff response was to call 911 and try to get the patient transferred to a general hospital with emergency services. A more recent study by the Inspector General found that only 55 of the 109 physician-owned specialty hospitals had emergency services and some even lacked an on-duty nurse or an on-call physician on the night shift (Lee, 2008).

Advocates for the development of physician-owned specialty hospitals argue that opponents just want to block competition which would help address the nation's healthcare problems. They point to studies that found that the functioning of general hospitals appeared to be largely unaffected by the presence of competing specialty hospitals and that the quality of care was at least comparable (Greenwald, Cromwell *et al.*, Government Accountability Office, 2006).

At the local community level, the debate over physician-owned specialty hospitals has often been even more bitter and heated. General community hospitals and hospital specialists have long been wary collaborators. Specialists have always played on the edge of competing directly with the hospitals where they have privileges by expanding the diagnostic and outpatient procedures they do in their own offices and outpatient surgical centers. Increasingly, restrictive payments by health plans have changed the calculus for specialists at the same time national firms began selling the idea of creating specialty hospitals to these physicians and assisting them in their construction. General community hospitals have waged their war against the threat posed by physician-owned specialty hospitals on multiple fronts. They have launched public relations campaigns that tout their strengths as a hospital services provider. Reluctant to directly confront their own hospital specialists with whom they must maintain a working relationship, they have relied on national, state and state hospital associations to push their legislative and legal case for blocking their development. Some general hospitals have offered their specialists joint ownership in for-profit ventures. Indeed, some of the physician owned specialty hospitals that have been developed are joint ventures with local general hospitals. In a few cases, they have openly battled with specialists by revoking or using the threat of revoking their hospital privileges (Abelson, 2004).

No one wants to be portrayed as being greedy in such battles and both sides have tried to stake out the higher ground. The push for "market-driven" solutions to healthcare's problems transformed the efforts of hospital specialists to carve out a larger piece of the healthcare dollar into a noble, even heroic, social mission. Harvard Business School professor, Regina Herzlinger's book, *Market Driven Health Care: Who*

Wins, Who Loses in the Transformation of America's Largest Service Industry, attracted a large following and received the Book of the Year Award from the American College of Health Executives in 1998 (Herzlinger, 1997). The basic message was, do not try to build seamless managed care or an integrated delivery system, just focus on providing a single service, such as hernia repair, angioplasty, or bariatric surgery. Compete in the market by designing an organization around the customers of that service. As healthcare is transformed in this way, it will improve customer satisfaction, enhance quality and reduce cost. Herzlinger went on to say that as a result of this transformation, healthcare will be provided, not by general practitioners and general hospitals, but by "focused factories." She concluded by emphasizing that physicians, the providers of services in these factories, must have a financial stake in their success.

One might question whether a Midas Muffler approach to healthcare really works, since health and illness are much more complex, but it was an easy idea to sell. It fit perfectly with the way surgical specialists are paid and their desire for greater control and more income. Physicians owned hospitals in many communities in the mid-20th century. Many of these hospitals had a shabby history of poor quality and financial abuse. Hospital reform efforts closed most of them down. Indeed, one could argue, it is hard enough to get a medical staff to exercise effective control over the privileges and quality of care provided by its members, much less when the medical staff member is also an owner of the hospital. Now a new version of this model was being promoted as the best way to reform healthcare. Professor Herzlinger testified at the Senate Committee for Homeland Security and Government Affairs hearings arguing for the lifting of the moratorium on Medicare contracting with new physician-owned specialty hospitals. The moratorium, she argued was:

> *"Based on a faulty diagnosis: specialty hospitals do not cause hospitals to lose their most profitable areas and physician ownership does not induce overuse of hospital services. ....As elsewhere in our economy, specialized healthcare facilities, partially owned*

> *by entrepreneurial physicians, present the hope for a higher qual-*
> *ity and higher productivity healthcare system. The specialization*
> *integrates care that consumers must now struggle to obtain from*
> *a system organized by separate providers and typically reduces*
> *costs. And ownership provides an important additional incentive*
> *for physicians to provide the best value for the money....Let us*
> *cure our healthcare woes the good, old-fashioned way, not with a*
> *thicket of regulations, but instead with a market of competitive*
> *suppliers — entrepreneurial physicians and other providers —*
> *and empowered consumers"*
>
> *(Herzlinger, 2006)*

Barix clinics combined a simple surgical solution to a growing health problem, and by doing so, took advantage of the increasing financial concerns of surgeons by embracing the noble vision of market driven reform.

Barix Clinics of Pennsylvania

The first for-profit specialty hospital entry into the Philadelphia market, Barix Clinics of Pennsylvania in Langhorne, Pennsylvania, opened in 2002. The hospital is located on the edge of what is called the "fat belt," the Pennsylvania Dutch area that stretches across the southeastern part of Pennsylvania that has the highest obesity rates in the state. It is where the traditional high-calorie Pennsylvania Dutch diet has remained, but the heavy physical labor capable of absorbing that intake of calories has disappeared.

Barix is a subsidiary of a privately held company based in Ypsilanti Michigan, Forest Health Services. It owns four other bariatric surgery facilities (two in Michigan, one in Illinois, and one in Ohio).

Barix Clinics was designed to meet the physical and emotional needs of their customers. Chairs throughout the facility are wider than normal and can comfortably hold somebody that weighs 700 pounds. Hospital gowns come supersized as do the hospital's stretchers and operating room tables. Even the bathrooms are built to accommodate the morbidly obese. The entire facility is geared towards larger patients.

On the obesityhelp.com website, 215 consumers of bariatric services at Barix Clinics of Pennsylvania gave generally glowing assessments of their care (obesityhelp, 2009). Some drove more than three hours to be cared for at the facility. Many were delighted with the attention to every detail that made it a comfortable place for an obese person to receive care. One said, "I wanted a hospital that understood what I was going through." Still another said, "The respect I receive here was hands down the best. You are made to feel comfortable and talked to like you are a human. Not some freak." The nursing staff and the doctors got rave reviews. The only criticisms concerning staff were related to rudeness and failure to return calls of some of the office staff.

Insurance coverage, however, was a big issue. "I am still waiting for my insurance company to accept the hospital in their network and I feel like I am being strung along," one said. Another felt that she got the run around from the office staff, who first said she had coverage and then eventually told her she had to go elsewhere. Still another said, "I decided against it after being told I was out of network and they would arrange a loan for surgery. I would be reimbursed by my insurance company but I was told the total was about $50,000. Since my insurance would only cover 80% I figured I'd go where it wasn't a money making proposition."

Barix Clinics of Pennsylvania provides no emergency service and all patients are scheduled elective admissions. Barix has fewer patients with serious chronic conditions than the local teaching hospitals that also perform the procedure. "Barix isn't cherry picking," one of the physicians insisted. "Patients with high risk for complications belong in a full-service hospital" (Goldstein, 2006).

The facility was initially staffed with the following full-time equivalents: 1 dietician, 1.2 inhalation therapists, 1 registered pharmacist, 9 RNs and 14 other personnel. As some of the comments from patients suggest, the relatively low volume of patients provides for personalized care that would not be possible in a larger general hospital.

The facility's medical staff includes four surgeons that form a group practice, Bariatric Specialists of Pennsylvania, PC which is affiliated with the hospital and specializes in providing medical services to severely overweight individuals.

More than 95% of Barix patients have commercial insurance. In 2005, Barix Clinics of Pennsylvania did 764 such surgeries, about a 33% market share in the region. Its volume continues to grow. The hospital provides essentially no uncompensated care and no care to Medicare or Medicaid patients. Most acute general hospitals rely on a substantial proportion of patients covered by Medicare and Medicaid and provide at least some uncompensated care. Net patient revenue in fiscal year 2007 was $13.6 million (PHC4, 2009). After operating at substantial losses in its first few years, the hospital essentially broke even (operating margin 0.6%). It would appear to be positioned to begin providing a return on the investment to its owners.

Discussion

- In the broader policy debate related to the development of for-profit specialty hospitals, how would you use the Barix Clinics case to support or alternatively oppose these developments?
- What key challenges does Barix Clinics face in ensuring its long term profitability?

Postscript

Perhaps the most complex and difficult aspect to assess concerning the future of Barix is how health plans will deal with the growing demand for bariatric surgery. Health plans do not worry about what happens in the long run. Individuals or their employers will change coverage. At best, they focus their coverage of preventive treatment on what will save money for them in terms of overall costs within three years. Bariatric surgery does not provide such a return on investment in this short time period. It costs about $25,000 and arguably could possibly return about $5,000 in savings a year (Avraham and Camara, 2007). Thus coverage of the procedure is generally limited to those that already have serious, life threatening conditions caused or complicated by morbid obesity. This puts specialty hospitals at a disadvantage, since they would prefer not to treat cases with complications and, a larger general hospital may be the more appropriate site for such cases. Moreover, when health plans contract with providers for discounted rates as part of a network of preferred providers, this is a costly process. The plans may be reluctant to enter into such contracts with highly specialized hospital providers who will serve few, if any, of their enrollees. This puts specialty hospitals such as Barix at a disadvantage in competing with larger general hospitals, as noted by the comment from one of their frustrated patients. It is not an accident that the new specialty hospitals are largely concentrated in areas of the country with low managed-care penetration rates.

Most health plans look to Medicare for direction in the reimbursement of new services. Up until 2006, Medicare covered bariatric surgery only if it was intended to correct an illness caused or aggravated by obesity. In 2006, Medicare expanded coverage of bariatric procedures, but only for those at a Center of Excellence as designated by the American Society of Bariatric Surgery or an American College of Surgeons Certified Level 1 Center for Bariatric Surgery. Most of these centers are based in larger general hospitals with teaching programs and none of the new specialty bariatric hospitals have this designation. The kind of additional and emergency services that such larger hospitals provide, in the judgment of these professional bodies, affords a greater degree of safety and, possibly as a result, lower malpractice risk. More than twenty short term hospitals in Pennsylvania alone are qualified for payments on this basis and this may increase the competition Barix clinics will face in providing services covered by private health plans. While physicians at Bariatric Clinics in Pennsylvania limit their practices to those under the age of 60 and the hospital apparently claims to have no interest in contracting with Medicare, it does set a standard that other insurers may follow. The puck may stop here and Barix Clinics may not have followed Gretsky's advice after all.

Discussion

- How could Bariatric Clinics address these potential health plan difficulties?

Case 11:   The Gift of the Heart

Background[10]

> Marilyn Rivers, 22, drank too much at the party after work, drove too fast and crashed into a concrete embankment on the way home. Her skull was crushed on impact. Marilyn was placed on artificial life support upon arrival at Lehigh Valley Medical Center and the nurse supervisor notified Debra Rose, the Delaware Valley Transplant Program coordinator on call. Debra arrived at the hospital 50 minutes later and entered the lobby where Marilyn's stunned parents stood in shock. Ushered into a nearby conference room and with the help of the attending physician, she explained the current status of their daughter and the choices that remained. She was brain dead and could be kept on life support for a short time. They could make the necessary arrangements with a funeral parlor or hold off on this and use her death to preserve another life, honoring the preference Marilyn had indicated on her driver's license. An hour later, Debra sat down in an adjacent office and logged on to the United Network for Organ Sharing (UNOS) database in Richmond, Virginia. She entered information from her assessment of Marilyn and then pressed enter. A few seconds later, the list of potential heart recipients, ranked in order of an algorithm as prescribed by a national consensus panel (blood match, time on the waiting list, medical urgency, and distance) spit out from her portable printer. George Mason was the first name on the list and she placed her first call, as protocol requires, to the Temple University contact for their transplant team.

---

[10] The author served as the chairperson of the southeastern Pennsylvania task force that reviewed criteria for approval of transplants programs in 1984. He interviewed many people involved in the organ procurement program, (now referred to as the "Gift of Life"), and observed and interviewed heart transplant team members and patients at Temple University Hospital. He is indebted to their cooperation and insights. The story that begins this case is a fictionalized distillation of these experiences.

A half hour later at 1:00 AM, George got the call from the hospital. "We have a donor, come on in." His overnight bag had been packed by his bed, ready to make this trip for almost two months. He and his family increasingly worried that the call would come too late. His wife drove him through the empty streets and they arrived at the hospital thirty minutes later.

Prepped and waiting on the operating table, he conversed casually with the members of the transplant team while they all waited for the call from Allentown. Only when the heart had been harvested, inspected and was en route by helicopter, would the sedation and preparatory surgery — opening the chest cavity — begin. George recounted the out-of-body experience that he had during his previous emergency heart surgery, watching himself on the operating table far below, lifted by a beam of light. He had turned his life around, had become a member of Alcoholics Anonymous (AA) and had been sober for three years. Like many transplant recipients, he would later try to make sense out the additional time he had been provided by connecting his life to the sketchy details of the life of the donor.[11]

The burning smell from the saw as it cut through his sternum and opened a foot-long incision in his chest permeated the operating room. His ribs were separated and the heart-lung machine took over, making it possible to remove the diseased heart and place the new one in position, re-attaching the blood vessels. His new heart failed to start beating and an anxious minute passed as electric shock (defibrillation) was applied. Once the blood was flowing through the new heart normally and checked for leaks, the

---

[11] George suffered from cardiomyopathy. Alcoholic cardiomyopathy is a disorder where excessive habitual drinking causes a weakening of the heart muscle so that it cannot pump blood efficiently. It is not readily distinguishable from other possible causes of cardiomyopathy, but alcohol consumption is assumed to play a role in many cases and probably did in George's case. Since cardiomyopathy is the most frequent condition that necessitates a heart transplant, fatal automobile crashes are the most frequent source of organs and alcohol consumption a frequent contributor to such crashes, the donor and the recipient in this case were indeed linked as is the overall demand for and supply of hearts.

*heart-lung machine was disconnected and the chest incision
closed. After more than four hours on the operating table, George
was carefully wheeled into the recovery room.*

*Several days later in a wheelchair, George attended his first
meeting of the Temple heart transplant support group in the large
auditorium on the first floor of the hospital. Over sixty heart recipients were in attendance. Most have returned to their normal lives
and most, with some care, will have close to a normal life
expectancy. The mood was lively and there was banter and
applause as they welcomed their newest member.*

The real story in this case, however, is not about George and the gift
he received, nor about the scientists and surgical pioneers who have made
that gift possible. While these stories have captured the imagination of the
public, the true gift of the heart is how it has illuminated the medical
marketplace and provided a parable, a microcosm of our history and the
choices we have made about the organization and financing of medical
care. The choices about heart transplantation have been vivid and stark.
They have forced the creation of a system of allocating care quite different
from that of the healthcare system as a whole, which has evolved more
haphazardly and with less debate and reflection about ethical issues
of equity.

In the 1980s, heart transplantation began to shift from a questionable
experimental procedure to an accepted form of treatment, and thus one
that third parties were willing to reimburse. The good results achieved by
a few university transplant teams and the introduction of cyclosporine
therapy to prevent organ rejection increased one year survival rates to
over 75%. Hearts are unlike kidneys, which can be preserved from 24 to
72 hours, thus allowing long distance distribution. Instead, hearts must
be transplanted within four hours, which limits travel times. The major
problem was supply. While transplant surgeons in a few regions, such
as Philadelphia, had set up regional cooperative organ procurement
services, in some areas, such as New York City, medical centers with
transplant programs ran their own services. Harvesting organs from their
own patients and sometimes getting into ambulance chases to accident
sites with competing organ procurement services were a bit unseemly.

In addition, there were other areas of the country where no organ procurement service existed at all. The National Transplant Act of 1984 (PL 98–507) prohibited the purchase of organs and provided grants for the establishment of regional organ procurement agencies and a national organ sharing system.

The general assumption in the United States was that harvested organs were all donated as gifts, just as the bulk of the blood supply had long been provided. However, disturbing advertisements and stories began to appear in the press. A Pulitzer prize-winning series of articles appearing in the Pittsburgh Press described the international network involved in the sale of kidneys from living unrelated donors and the queue jumping of a wealthy foreign national in exchange for a large gift to the local transplant hospital (Schneider and Flaherty, 1985). These stories helped spur the implementation of the Department of Health and Human Services task force recommendations to develop a national system of organ sharing and standardized criteria for allocating organs (Task Force on Organ Transplantation, 1986). The earlier bill and the recommendations of the task force ended competing organ services and established a regionalized network covering all areas of the United States. The creation of this network was driven by very practical concerns. Those regions with a single organ procurement service, such as Philadelphia, had a far better "harvest rate." Everyone saw increasing the organ supply as the most critical problem. Allocating the available supply became based on objective standardized national criteria. Subjective criteria, such as assessments of social support and lifestyle, were eliminated. (In the past, George Mason's prior alcoholism could have disqualified him for consideration as a recipient by some transplant programs.) The goal was to make it objective, transparent and something everyone — donors, potential recipients and surgeons, could understand. This produced the algorithm in the UNOS computerized national database used to select George Mason to receive the heart of Marilyn Rivers.

What is striking, however, was that these decisions, which created a new regulatory system and eliminated market competition between transplant procurement organizations as well as between transplant recipients, happened in the midst of Reagan Administration efforts to promote the free market in healthcare. Once the decision was made to close the Pandora's Box of the sale of organs to the highest bidder, the rest followed.[12] It followed because, since organs could be distributed only as a voluntary gift, it was not the surgeons or those with wealth or political connections that had the ultimate power. Instead, it was the general public, those with the organs that had the power. Create a system of organ allocation that is perceived to be unfair, that benefits only the rich and powerful, and the supply of hearts would shrivel. As a consequence, there has been a very concerted effort to maintain at least the perception of fairness and equity, if not the reality. The system developed to supply organs and allocate them to patients in the United States has done a good job of assuring such a perception. What was left unresolved and is still bitterly contested is: who should do the transplants?

The Philadelphia Story: Who Should Do Heart Transplants?

Taking hearts now considered a gift to be allocated on the basis of equity and fairness and placing them within the emerging healthcare market place of Philadelphia in the 1980s, was indeed like placing a round peg into a square hole. The problem was the perception that being a facility that did heart transplants was of critical symbolic importance in assuring the long term financial survival of cardiovascular surgical programs in an increasingly competitive market. In 1984, fixed price payment per admission adjusted for case mix (Diagnostic Related Group or DRG payment) replaced the cost reimbursement formulas that had existed in the Medicare and state Medicaid program since 1966. While total admissions remained constant in the Philadelphia area, average length-of-stay dropped almost 10% and occupancy almost 8% (Smith and Pickard, 1986). Occupancy rates of some community hospitals dropped even more as the new excess capacity attracted physicians and patients to the prestigious institutions

---

[12] That box has never been fully closed and every year there are uncomfortable reminders of this. For example, a kidney ring kingpin nicknamed "Dr. Horror" is currently on trial in India as as the mastermind of a network with clients in Europe, Asia, the Middle East and the United States. See: Bhattacharjee, Y. (2008). Caveat Donor: A Street Brawl in India Brings Down a Global Kidney-Transplant Ring. *Atlantic*: 29–30.

that were perceived to be more on the "cutting edge" of medical break-throughs. The fear of the smaller community hospitals was that their insti-tutions over time would be relegated to one of the "have-nots" in terms of payment and prestige, essentially a facility providing predominantly non-acute services and serving as a nursing home or a drug rehab center (Griffith and White, 2006).

The first couple of years of the new payment system were profitable ones for the hospitals in the Philadelphia area. They had effectively responded to the new incentives by reducing length-of-stay and they sought ways to invest in new or expanded services that would ensure their long term future as a high-tech acute care "have." Hospitals began to look very closely at which physicians were contributing the most through their admissions to their bottom line and cardiovascular surgeons were by far the largest contributors. The surgeons knew this and a bidding war broke out among hospitals as they attempted to increase their volume of cardiovascular surgery by raiding the cardiovascular surgeons of their competitors.

Healthcare in the Philadelphia area thus arrived at an important water-shed in 1985. Pennsylvania still had a regional planning process based on the assumption that one could control use and cost by limiting the number of hospital beds, costly diagnostic equipment, and programs ensuring that medical needs were met and there would be no excess capacity. The mechanisms for achieving this was a process called Certificate of Need (CON). Hospitals wishing to expand services or capacity had to go through an elaborate review process that involved approval by the Philadelphia Health Systems Agency (HSA), the designated regional planning body and finally, a state decision to issue a CON. Lacking that approval, Medicare, Medicaid, and most private insurance plans would not pay for these services. In addition, a hospital that circumvented the process could not get bond or bank loan financing. It could also, conceiv-ably, lose its license to operate. One of the unstated and perhaps unin-tended functions of the CON process, was to provide a cross subsidy to city hospitals that cared for most of the poor. Thus, awarding a "franchise" for a highly profitable service, such as open-heart surgery, to a hospital that provided a lot of free care to indigents would help to ensure their financial viability.

Pushing against these cumbersome restrictions were the internal strategic planning efforts of every hospital in the area. Most assumed that in the new environment (the Reagan administration and the new payment mechanisms), the days of regional planning restrictions on the free market were numbered. Everyone recognized that by far the most profitable service line to develop or expand was cardiovascular surgery. Cardiovascular surgery had gone through remarkable breakthroughs in the last decade, developing many new procedures for mending damaged hearts and extending the lives of patients. New procedures are reimbursed at roughly what they cost when they are first introduced and those costs are never adjusted downward as hospitals as surgeons learn how to do the procedure more efficiently. Thus as new procedures become more common, they also become increasingly profitable.

If every hospital was going to try to develop a cardiovascular surgery service, how could a hospital ensure that their service would attract enough volume to be profitable and survive? The "answer" most of the larger hospitals concluded was to get the "jewel" for the "crown" of cardiovascular surgery, a heart transplant program. This highly visible, dramatic and emotionally charged program would cement their reputation in the eyes of the medical community and the general public as a pre-eminent center for cardiovascular care.

Temple University Hospital had submitted a "stealth" CON heart transplant application ahead of other potential competitors and before the Philadelphia Health Systems Agency (HSA) had begun to think systematically about the criteria for approving transplant programs. Immediately after Temple's transplant program had received its CON, the HSA was deluged with almost 20 CON applications for organ transplant programs (heart, liver, lung, kidney, etc.). Rather than acting on these applications individually, the agency imposed a moratorium on new organ transplant CON reviews, pending a systematic review and the establishment of guidelines. For the Hospital of the University of Pennsylvania, Hahnemann, Jefferson and Einstein and their prospective transplant surgeons, anxious that Temple not build up too much of head start, this was infuriating. They arrived at the meetings of the advisory group, in the conference room of the HSA in Philadelphia, fuming.

The problem of developing criteria for approving new transplant programs was different from the typical reviews involving the acquisition of costly state-of-the-art equipment to diagnose or treat patients. Just as the introduction of high-speed Xerox machines in offices had exploded the number of copies made to take advantage of the capacity of these new machines, so had the number of diagnostic and treatment procedures in a medical setting expanded to take advantage of its newly acquired equipment. This "Xerox effect" could greatly increase the cost of healthcare by increasing its use in cases where it was of questionable value. None of this was a problem for heart transplants. The supply of organs was unlikely to increase. Indeed, if effective preventive measures (e.g. seat belts, motorcycle helmets, DUI and speed law enforcement) were put in place, the supply might even decline. In addition, the organ allocation process did a good job, arguably better than for any other medical service, in assuring that this limited resource would be allocated only to those who needed it the most.

The problem in the case of heart transplant programs and most of the other organ transplant programs was, "what is the magic number?" How many transplants does a transplant center need to do a good job? For example, assume that in the Philadelphia region roughly eighty hearts are harvested each year. Is it better to have one transplant program that does eighty or ten programs that do an average of eight transplants a year?

In healthcare, perhaps the oldest and most consistently documented relationship is between the volume of procedures done and outcomes. The more of a particular procedure a physician does, such as coronary artery bypass graft (CABG), percutaneous coronary interventions (PCT) and bariatric surgery, the better the outcomes (fewer deaths, complications, readmissions, etc.). Acting on such assumptions, the Business Roundtable Leapfrog group, which represents major purchasers of health insurance, has suggested minimum volumes for surgeons who perform procedures: 100 CABG, 75 PCI and 20 bariatric procedures per year (Leapfrog Group, 2007). The overall volume of procedures done in a hospital has also been found to be related to outcomes and the Business Roundtable has suggested minimum volumes as a proxy for quality in selecting hospitals, such as at least 450 CABGs per year and neonatal intensive care units providing care for at least 50 very low birth weight babies a year (Leapfrog Group, 2008).

The use of such numbers as a proxy for quality remains politically and empirically controversial. There are some high volume providers that have poor outcomes and low volume ones that have good outcomes.

The most commonly used argument for volume requirements is that "practice makes perfect," and that a surgeon and a hospital need to do a certain number of procedures a year to learn how to do them right and to maintain their proficiency. This is the "learning curve" idea. In manufacturing, it has been used to estimate the cost of production of airplanes, boxes, candy and many other things. The general rule-of-thumb is that with every doubling of the number of units produced, the labor costs per unit will decline, on average by about 20%. In the Temple transplant program, the proportion of patients not surviving one year after transplant dropped from 50% after the first eight transplants to less than 25% after the first sixteen, or a 50% decline in death rates, but the average charges per transplant dropped less than 10% (Smith and Larson, 1989). In other words, the transplant team "learned" quickly how to save lives, but little of this translated into any cost savings. This is partly because of the way surgeons and hospitals are paid. If the learning curve explains the better outcomes of high volume programs, then perhaps the fewer surgical teams doing heart transplants the better the quality and, possibly, for a little lower cost.

However, there are at least three other plausible explanations for the relationship between volume and outcomes and each suggest a somewhat different conclusion about how many heart transplant programs to permit.

First, the high volume center could be the consequence of patients and their referring physicians knowing which center has the best outcomes. The conclusion then might be that the market is indeed working, and we do not have to worry about how many transplant programs we permit in Philadelphia. The good programs will succeed and the bad ones will fail.

Second, another plausible explanation would be that high volume centers can afford to be more selective about the cases that they take. They can avoid taking on the higher risk and more complicated cases and the ones lacking more desirable insurance plans because they have more than enough business to keep the transplant team busy. For example, non-whites, Medicaid patients and the uninsured operated on for complex surgical procedures were less likely to receive these procedures in high volume hospitals (Liu, Zingmond *et al.*, 2006) . If this is indeed the case, it would certainly present a dilemma. More programs would mean that more high risk and questionable cases would get on the waiting list. Fewer programs would mean fewer minorities and persons with less adequate or desirable health insurance would have a chance to get a transplant.

Finally, another plausible explanation would be that the higher volume centers are financially healthier and this translates into better staffing and more resources that produce better outcomes. The volume required to break even in such a program is high, since the staffing and other resources that need to be dedicated to it are substantial. For example, when the Temple heart transplant program celebrated its 100th transplant, more than 100 heart transplant "team members" showed up for the celebration. If the financial viability of the program explained the better outcomes in higher volume complex surgical programs, then one should either restrict the number of programs or find a way to return to a cost based reimbursement system.

What makes the decision difficult is that all four of these different explanations probably contribute to the volume-outcome relationship. Ultimately, the question is how does one decide how many heart transplant programs to permit in the Philadelphia area?

As a part of its proceedings, the HSA transplant task force met with transplant program experts outside of the Philadelphia area and polled most of the major transplant programs across the country by telephone. How many transplants do you believe need to be done a year to assure a high quality program? Those queried had almost as much difficulty with the question as the members of the task force. Not knowing what else to do, the task force tallied up the numbers the programs gave and took the average.

At the final meeting of the task force, the room was packed. As the organ transplant volume calculations were removed from an envelope and announced by its chairman, the proceeding took on some of the tension and drama of an Academy Awards ceremony: "The annual volume of heart transplants required of a new program is......12."

Discussion

- Assuming that about 80 hearts continue to be harvested for transplants each year in the region, what are roughly the number of transplant programs that can be approved and reasonably be expected to meet the requirement of at least 12 transplants a year?

• A single program could accommodate 80 transplants a year. Should the region be limited to one program? Should it just be left up to the free market to decide with no regional restrictions placed on the number of heart transplant programs approved? Explain your reasoning.

Postscript

Federal funding ended and the Philadelphia Health Systems Agency shut up shop in January 1988, leaving the area hospitals and state government to muddle through. The CON restrictions on open-heart surgery and transplant programs at the state level remained in effect for another eight years, adopting most of the minimum number requirements hastily pulled together by the Philadelphia area HSA organ transplant task force. CON requirements in Pennsylvania ended in 1996. Several politically influential suburban hospitals interested in establishing open-heart surgery programs helped push the termination of CON in the state legislature. Since then, the number of hospitals in the Philadelphia region doing coronary artery bypass graph (CABG) procedures increased from 11 to 21, while the total number of these procedures declined 23% (Stark and Goldstein, 2003). Most of the new CABG programs were developed by suburban hospitals that cater predominantly to a more affluent privately insured market. Only five hospitals in the region meet the minimally acceptable number of CABG procedures per year (450) once required for a CON. There are now seven hospitals with heart transplant programs in the Philadelphia area. In 2007, only two hospitals with the largest endowments to support such an arms race performed more than 12 transplants (Hospital of the University of Pennsylvania 54, Jefferson University Hospital 16). As the number of heart transplant programs as a whole in the United States has increased, the number of heart transplants done in the Philadelphia area hospitals has declined.

Temple University Hospital, which in total has still done more transplants in the region than any other program (885), exceeded by only four transplant centers nationwide, did only five transplants in 2007. In 1997, perhaps before the impact of the termination of CON could take effect, the

Temple heart transplant program had done 82. About 500 of the Temple transplant recipients are still living and many continue to participate in Temple's heart transplant alumni support group. In 2007, the Medicare program finalized the requirement that, in their efforts to ensure that Medicare beneficiaries receive the highest quality of care, a condition of participation for heart transplant programs would be that they do a minimum of ten transplants a year. Temple's heart transplant program, which has performed less than ten transplants a year over the last three years, faced a May 2009 deadline to either increase its numbers or be terminated from the Medicare program (Goldstein, 2008). According to the UNOS database, as of November 1, 2008 there were only four patients on Temple's list awaiting transplants. One of the other heart transplant programs in Philadelphia, unable to maintain adequate volume, shut down in November 2008. Temple may soon follow, but the mystery of the gift of the heart and the lessons that gift offers for the organization and financing of healthcare in the United States will remain.

> George Mason was persistent, "I just want to thank them." The gift is a strictly anonymous one. Much red tape and soul searching within the organ procurement network followed. Finally asked, Marilyn River's mother said, "Yes, we'd like that." They met at a diner half-way between Philadelphia and Allentown. It was awkward at first and they talked about the weather, their trip to the diner and the prospects for the Phillies baseball team. Just as they were about to part, Marilyn's father said, "There is one thing my wife and I would like to do before we go" and he made a motion. George nodded and smiled. In turn, Marilyn's father and mother knelt down and pressed their ear against George's chest. They heard the beat and smiled back.

Discussion

- What lessons about the organization and financing of healthcare do you take from the experience of heart transplant programs in the United States?

7

Forecasting Trends and Repackaging the Future

Repackaging Care

"Nothing ever changes but the packaging," an advertising executive once told me. All the basic components of healthcare — prevention, diagnosis, medications, procedures and chronic care stay the same. The "repackaging" reconfigures these components to adapt to technological and demographic changes. The "repackagers" include private entrepreneurs and public policymakers responding to these shifts.

The most significant technological shift shaping such repackaging is the World Wide Web. For good or ill, it has taken the distribution of health related information out of the hands of providers and globalized it. Both healthcare regulators and service providers are struggling to catch up. The average patient now arrives at his or her doctor's office armed with detailed information downloaded from the internet about real or imagined conditions, while the medical practice has yet to convert to electronic medical records. Only about 10% of medical practices in the United States have fully functioning electronic medical records systems. This long heralded, but delayed transformation has proved easier to implement in less fragmented market-oriented systems of care. While most private practices have no way of quickly identifying and notifying patients about potentially life threatening side-effects of prescribed medications that have recently come to light, most federally qualified neighborhood health centers, designed for low income people lacking access to private primary care, have the capacity in their electronic record keeping system to do this in just a few key strokes. The Veteran's Administration Health System, our largest safety net provider, serves as the model for what fully integrated electronic medical records in a nationwide system of hospitals and outpatient services can do. In terms of the capacity of electronic medical records systems to ensure the safety and quality of care provided for patients, the private practice care for the more affluent in this country lags behind that provided to the medically indigent, as well as patients in most European countries.

Patients in the U.S., however, find ways to work around the lags in the electronic sophistication of their medical providers. An increasing number of patients fill prescriptions over the internet seeking the best prices worldwide. This, as Case 12 illustrates, opens up a black market that exposes consumers to the same risks that existed more than one hundred years ago before all the legal protections were developed in the drug industry and the distribution of medications. Akhil Bansal, a business school student with ambitions, became the focus of the first major bust in this new drug war and was sentenced to thirty years in prison as a result.

The most significant demographic shift shaping the repackaging of healthcare is the aging of the U.S. population. The proportion of the population over 65 will increase 58% between 2000 and 2030 (Centers for Disease Control, 2003). This should shift resources towards caring for chronic disease to support a growing frail elderly population. Such services are more dependent on state and local public dollars and the invisible "informal care system" patched together by families and friends than on acute care services. The private long term care insurance market continues to cover the costs of only a small fraction of this care. Since public dollars are increasingly squeezed, the financial viability of a long term care provider and the quality of the services they can offer are increasingly determined by their ability to attract those that can afford to pay for such services out of their pockets. Case 13 describes these dynamics as they play out for Paul Klaassen and the company he founded, Sunrise Senior Living, Inc. that would grow to become the nation's largest developer and manager of assisted living facilities.

Both Case 12 and Case 13 illustrate the dark underbelly of such repackaging and the fragility of progress. Case 12 returns us to the edge of the patent medicine free market abuses that existed before 20th century reforms. Case 13 moves us full circle back to the 19th century world of poor houses where the elderly were punished for being chronically ill, poor and lacking family that could care for them. Real progress is illusive and the repackaging may conceal a less attractive future. Perhaps more fundamental repackaging is in order.

Case 12: Globalization, Bansal and the Internet Prescription Bust[13]

Background

The front page of the *Philadelphia Inquirer* for Sunday, November 19, 2006, featured the story of the criminal investigation of a Temple University Healthcare Management MBA student. Akhil Bansal, M.D. had been arrested a month before graduation in April 2006 for operating an internet network illegally selling prescription drugs that grossed at least $8 million (Shiffman, 2007). A twenty-six year old Indian-trained physician, he had plans after graduation to acquire two legitimate medical transcription businesses. On December 14, 2007, he was sentenced to thirty years in prison.

In 2006, prescription drug expenditures in the United States accounted for $216 billion dollars. It has been the most rapidly expanding component of healthcare costs for several decades. While the U.S. accounts for only 5% of the population of the world, it accounts for almost half the prescription drug sales. Prices for prescription drugs are substantially higher in the United States than in other countries. Government group purchasing in most other countries has forced manufacturers to offer deep discounts. Also, the manufacture and sale of cheaper knock-offs of patented prescription medicines is less tightly controlled in most other countries. The pharmaceutical industry argues that the rest of the world is not paying its fair share of the cost of the development of new drugs. Industry critics argue that the pharmaceutical industry support in Congress exploits U.S. consumers, forcing them to pay more. In either case, the situation creates an incentive for U.S. consumers to seek drugs

---

[13] The information in this case relies on an excellent investigative series published in 2007 in the Philadelphia Inquirer written by staff writer John Shiffman. See: http://www.philly. com/inquirer/special/pill/ for the full account.

elsewhere and an opportunity for internet pharmacies with illegal or marginally legal suppliers outside the U.S. to make large profits.

In addition, the distinction between over-the-counter medications (those that a consumer can purchase directly) and prescription medications (those that require the oversight and control by medical practitioners) differs markedly between countries, with the U.S. exercising more restrictive control than most. In India, and in most other developing nations, with the possible exception of narcotics, there is little restriction in terms of what medications can be purchased over the counter. Even in the U.S., the notion of prescription control on drugs is relatively new. The Food and Drug Administration did not begin to exercise control over drugs by requiring physician prescription until the 1940s.

In spite of efforts to curtail it, a persistent "grey market" exists in the internet purchase of prescriptions by U.S. residents in the neighboring countries of Canada and Mexico. In Canada, the national health plan negotiates deep discounts with pharmaceutical firms. In Mexico, prices have had to match the lower standard of living in order to sell and there is more tolerance for lower price knock-offs of drugs still protected by company patents. The limited coverage of prescription drugs by health insurance plans drives consumers to seek lower price alternatives from internet pharmacies. The internet pharmacies include thousands of constantly changing sites, some complying with all of the practice and patient safety standards of the National Association of Boards of Pharmacies and some clearly violating state and national laws.

In addition, the growth of internet sales of pharmaceuticals has occurred during a profound shift in the relationship between providers of healthcare and their patients. Providers acknowledge that care has become more "consumer directed" and patients in most settings are now at least equal partners in treatment decisions. This paradigm shift was reflected in the loosening of FDA restrictions in 1997 on direct marketing of prescription medications to consumers. Pharmaceutical firms have invested heavily in television and other forms of direct advertising of prescription medications and it has helped to produce substantial increases in sales. One could also argue that it has encouraged self-medication and the growth of a grey market, as well as illegal internet prescription sales.

The growth of the consumer directed ethic and internet sales of pharmaceuticals is part of the globalization of business in general. Globalization means using the advantage of manufacturing products in less developed countries with the lowest labor and regulatory costs and then selling them in developed countries for much higher prices. Businesses and business schools have embraced such practices enthusiastically and with little criticism. Starting in the 1990s, Temple University, like other business schools, expanded its offerings in international business and began providing a specialized International MBA. The international business courses at Temple provided much encouragement of global entrepreneurial thinking with a less questioning view of the legal and ethical issues concerning these developments than was perhaps warranted. Although Akhil Bansal was by no means helplessly swept along by these patterns of thinking in his MBA training program into a serious crime, perhaps Temple's MBA program lacked critical balance about these new kinds of business opportunities.

The Business Plan

The plan had been to earn an MBA in healthcare financial management in Philadelphia, but family ties and the opportunity for large profits drew Akhil into an extracurricular global business venture. As an Indian and an only son, he acquiesced to his father's wishes and began financially helping the family by receiving knock-off pills from India and then re-shipping them from inside the United States. His sister, back in India, served as marketing director for this venture, producing some of the familiar spam that floods the internet.

> *Sir,*
> *We wish to introduce ourselves as wholesale distributor and supplier of generic and branded medicines manufactured by top multinational pharmaceutical companies of India. We can drop ship to your customers in U.S. 100% delivery without any customs problems.*
> *We charge the following generic: Viagra $1; Valium $60.00 per 100 tabs; codeine $50 per 100 tabs...*
> *Let me know if you are interested.*
> *Thanks and regards,*
> *Julie.*

There were soon responses from pharmaceutical website retailers, most operating outside the boundaries of the U.S. Akhil's job was to retrieve the concealed bulk shipments of generic pills from India in Philadelphia and repackage them for shipment to individual customers in the U.S. The volume grew. Akhil's father put him in touch with an Indian couple in Queens, New York who would handle the shipping for the growing business. In their basement, newly arrived Indian immigrants earned $6 an hour repackaging and relabeling the pills.

The business began to take on the trappings of a multinational corporation for which Akhil served as chief executive officer. He traveled to New York in a new business suit and red "power tie" to make a persuasive PowerPoint marketing presentation to close a deal with the operator of a large volume pharmaceutical web site based in Ft. Lauderdale, Florida. That PowerPoint presentation would later be used as key evidence in his conviction.

In less than a year, the business had grown from a two person, part-time operation shipping 1,000 pills-a-day to a ten person, 50,000 pills-a-day operation. Akhil had earned his first million dollars and bought a luxury five bedroom condo in an affluent suburb of Delhi.

It was a business that ignored national boundaries. An order for a 110 tablets of Alprazolam, a generic sedative, from a 19-year old customer living in the King of Prussia suburb of Philadelphia would be first processed through an online pharmacy in Romania. His purchase would then be approved by a credit card processor in the British Channel Islands and then e-mailed to Indian suppliers in Agra, India. The Indian suppliers would add the order to the bulk shipment of medications forwarded to the rented home in Queens, New York, where an Indian supervisor printed it out and handed it to another Indian woman who took the 110 tablets out of a cubbyhole, slid the pills into an envelope, labeled it, and bagged it for pickup by UPS. Two days later, the requested drugs would arrive at the doorstep of the 19-year old in King of Prussia, Pennsylvania. Akhil's operation had expanded to include a dozen online pharmacies in all corners of the globe.

The Investigation

The Drug Enforcement Administration (DEA) is responsible for prosecuting the illegal distribution of prescription medicines in the United States.

In 2004, it was unprepared to effectively police the colossal growth of the internet prescription business. While it was obvious that any kid with a credit card and internet access could order addictive medications from the safety of home, the DEA so far, had only limited success in prosecuting rogue internet pharmacies. Congress was pressing the DEA to do something and the Akhil case which they had stumbled upon became their first major international effort to crackdown on illegal internet pharmacies. The agency needed to make a strong statement with a successful prosecution.

The investigation had begun almost a year earlier with the discovery of some suspicious packages by Airborne Express at the Philadelphia airport. Inside the packages, the supervisor found 120 tablets of generic Valium and knock-off Viagra. They tracked the packages to an ex-con in Chester, Pennsylvania who had been hired by Akhil to collect the shipment. The trail then led to Akhil, to the newly established distribution center in Queens, to Akhil's father in Agra, India, and then to their internet pharmaceutical website customers in Fort Lauderdale and Sarasota, Florida, Rochester, New York, San Jose, Costa Rica, Toronto, Canada, and Perth, Australia. Akhil was at the center of a new kind of drug dealer, supplier, and distribution network. From the DEA's perspective, he was "Mr. Big," the drug kingpin. There were now suspects on four continents, tens of thousands of U.S. customers and a network that represented a clear and growing threat to the health and safety of the U.S. public.

The challenge for the DEA was to match the technical sophistication and international collaboration of their target. DEA's software, developed to tap email initially crashed, overloaded by the volume arriving in Akhil's account from drug website customers. The DEA, FBI and the IRS all became involved. They were joined by India's Narcotics Control Bureau (NCB). The NCB placed a wire-tap on the phone of Akhil's father. A physician, Akhil's father had a license to dispense medicine in India and an export license, but this did not allow him to ship pills to the U.S.

From the wire-tap on Akhil's father, they heard him objecting to Akhil about his plan to sell customer data to spammers who would then use the information to follow-up on pill customers, some of whom had become addicts, pushing them to buy more. "It's America…Everything is for sale," Akhil argued.

While this investigation progressed, Akhil's business continued to expand. In a single week in March 2006, it had sold 54,590 Valium,

73,130 sleeping and 104,270 anti-anxiety pills. Akhil, however, wanted to get out of the business and move on. His father was ill and he was squabbling with his sister over control of the business. He wanted to finish his degree at Temple and use the profits from the operation to purchase two U.S. medical transcription services for about $700,000. He planned to outsource the transcription to lower cost workers in India, and take advantage of the time differences to provide next morning turnaround.

At the DEA's Special Operations Division outside of Washington, a meeting to coordinate the global take-down of Akhil's internet prescription network put the finishing touches on the plan to capture all of those involved in the drug distribution network. Timing was critical and the arrests of about twenty people in Philadelphia, Washington, New York, India, Costa Rica and Hungary had to be carried out simultaneously, along with the seizure of bank accounts in eleven countries. The sweep would begin at dawn on the East Coast on April 19, 2006.

The take-down plan, however, began to unravel. Pursuing his own independent investigation, New York State's Attorney General, Elliot Spitzer (he would later serve briefly as governor of New York before his involvement as a client of a Washington call-girl service would force his resignation), busted one of Akhil's larger on-line pharmacy clients in Rochester, New York. The Feds had urged him to hold off, but Spitzer made the arrest anyway and publicized it. Late in the evening of April 18th, Akhil got word of the arrest, discovered that his bank accounts had been frozen and panicked. At 1:30 AM on April 19th, he loaded his belongings in a friend's car to flee to Canada. They got less than one hundred yards down the road. The FBI agent, who had Akhil's apartment under surveillance, swerved his car in front of them, blocking their escape and aimed a pistol at Akhil.

The Conviction

The trial lasted four weeks. Akhil's defense attorney argued that it was a case about "a legitimate businessman who used the technology at his disposal to fill a niche in the marketplace." The prosecution presented a host of incriminating emails, invoices and bank records. Some of the website operators testified for the prosecution. The jury quickly convicted Akhil on 19 counts of drug trafficking and money laundering. On December 14, 2007, Akhil was sentenced to 30 years in jail by the U.S. District Court in Philadelphia. Judge Paul Diamond said at the sentencing, "The evidence of your guilt is overwhelming sir. You distributed poison throughout the country." Prior to sentencing, Akhil Bansal had argued, "Truly in my heart, I believe I did not commit these serious charges. I am studying the law and I ask myself every day, 'How did I end up here?'" He indicated that he planned to appeal his conviction. His defense attorney argued that he had been demonized by his own stubbornness and apparent arrogance in the courtroom and that he did what he did because he grew up in a strict Indian family and wished to please his father. The prosecutors challenged this view, arguing that Akhil was a greedy criminal who knew he was breaking the law. "Not once in this courtroom did he ever express remorse that anyone could have been harmed by what he did," said the prosecutor. As a medical school graduate in India, he was clearly in a position to understand his action, the prosecutor argued.

Discussion

- Given the shifting global nature of healthcare, what additional arguments could you make for and against Akhil's guilt? Should he have received a shorter or longer sentence?
- The internet has greatly expanded the information and options available for the individual healthcare consumer by erasing national boundaries. As this case illustrates, the creation of such a global market poses risks. It also offers benefits (e.g. lower costs, greater choice, more information to judge the quality and appropriateness of healthcare products and services, etc.). How can such a resource be regulated to best balance such risks and benefits?

Case 13: Aging, Klaassen and the Killer Application

Background

In 1981, Paul Klaassen and his wife Terri sold their house and moved into a boarded up nursing home. During the next twenty seven years, Klaassen became the key leader and visionary in the transformation of long term care in the United States. In the language of a similar transformation in consumer electronics, he had created a "killer application." That application took full advantage of the evolving organizational and financial pathologies of the long term care system in the U.S. and the shifting demographic realities of the market for long term care.

Just like the packaging of services in healthcare, consumer electronic products have a life cycle. A "killer application" combines what was previously done by different products into a single application that is cheaper, faster and more desirable. For example, newer model cell phones incorporate video, text messaging, music player and email functions that make the older models obsolete. These cycles of "creative destruction," celebrated as the essence of progress in a free market economy, leave a clutter of abandoned products in our closets (Schumpeter, 1975).

The packaging of services in healthcare in the United States, however, has followed just the opposite evolutionary path of creative destruction over the last century. Unlike consumer electronics, this path has produced increasingly differentiated and specialized services. This helped to create the opportunity that Klaassen was able to exploit.

Most hospitals, up until about 1910, were undifferentiated social welfare institutions. Their inhabitants included the frail elderly, the mentally and physically ill, and the homeless. Over the next two decades, acute care hospitals emerged as doctors' workshops focused on the short term treatment of acute illness, increasingly for paying patients. The indigent and those requiring long term care were off-loaded to county almshouses and poor farms as well as voluntary institutions that provided such care.

In the 1930s, the Great Depression forced a shift in the care of the elderly indigent from voluntary and county institutions or "indoor relief" to "outdoor relief." That is, instead of directly providing shelter and food, welfare programs would just provide cash assistance and individuals could acquire food and shelter on their own. The long held concern that such outdoor relief would encourage indigence was overcome by the magnitude of the issues that made indoor relief impractical. These issues included scandals surrounding conditions in the county facilities for their increasingly elderly residents and the political shift resulting in the passage of the Social Security legislation. Old Age Assistance (OAA), a part of that legislation, provided states with a 50% federal match for cash assistance to the indigent elderly. It gave the states a lot of flexibility in how they would operate the program and it would later serve as the model for the Medicaid legislation. *However, the Social Security legislation prohibited OAA payments to anyone living in a "public institution."* Since no local welfare administrators wanted to be stuck with having to pay these costs, most of these facilities were shut down. In their place, local welfare administrators sought shelter for their frail elderly charges in private boarding homes. The private boarding homes were typically large homes converted by their owners who needed to supplement their income. An unanticipated consequence was that these "ma and pa" homes would evolve into the current proprietary nursing home sector that now accounts for more than two-thirds of all nursing homes in the United States (Kaiser Family Foundation, 2008).

The passage of the Medicare and Medicaid legislation in 1965 produced a new wave of creative destruction. Medicare and Medicaid function as medical not social insurance programs, restricting payments to medically necessary care in medically appropriate facilities. Many of the older "ma and pa" boarding homes did not meet these standards and closed. Adding nursing home beds was not a financially or socially attractive option for acute-care hospitals and most chose not to do it. Medicare and Medicaid payments made acute care profitable, but the cost structure of acute hospitals and Medicaid nursing home payments made providing nursing home care by a hospital financially problematic. Also, Title VI of the 1964 Civil Rights Act was strictly enforced for hospitals and their nursing home units, but left free-standing nursing homes untouched by these racial integration efforts (Smith, 1999). This may have also contributed to the distinctive separation of acute hospital care from nursing home care that took place in the United States.

Yet, the promise of new federal Medicare and Medicaid funding attracted many real estate developers and entrepreneurs. Publicly-traded nursing home chains became one of the hottest stock investments (Stevenson, 2007). While in 1966, there were only a few publicly traded nursing home chains, by 1970 there were 90. They promised investors returns of 20–25% a year and, in many cases, went public before they had constructed a single facility. Reflecting a sequence of events that would repeat with Sunrise and the rest of the publicly traded assisted-living industry in 2007, unrealistic expectations, poor management and some notorious cases of fraud produced a precipitous decline in stock prices of these publicly traded nursing home chains in 1971. Nevertheless, these publicly traded nursing home chains helped produce a massive construction boom. Nursing home bed capacity in the United States increased more than fifty percent between 1963 and 1973, expanding to 1,174,900 beds, and exceeded the bed capacity of hospitals in the United States (National Center for Health Statistics, 1975). However, this "modern" nursing home sector neither offered the home-like environment of some of the older, more attractive boarding homes nor provided effective integration into the mainstream of medical practice and acute hospitals. In essence, the new federal funding had produced a return to indoor relief.

Thus, what had begun one hundred years ago as undifferentiated social welfare institutions had been transformed into a fragmented specialized collection of institutions which were divided into medical ones relying on federal health insurance and non-medical ones relying on the personal income of residents and cash assistance provided them by state welfare programs. The non-medical facilities could provide shelter, meals and assistance with daily living but were increasingly restricted by their licensure in providing medical services. The medical ones could provide medical services, but were increasingly restricted in terms of what Medicare, Medicaid and other health plans would pay for in providing shelter, meals and personal assistance. A true "killer application" in long term care would need to follow the path of consumer electronics and invent a way to combine both functions, doing them both better in a less costly and more attractive setting.

The Klaassen Assisted-Living Model

Klaassen's vision and how it differed from the traditional care model is summarized in Fig. 7.1. The traditional medical model organizes services in a way that is most convenient for physicians and other providers.

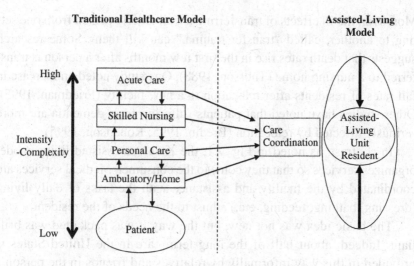

Fig. 7.1. The Traditional Healthcare Model vs The Assisted-Living Model.

The patient travels to them. Each setting is organized to provide a particular set of services along a "continuum of care." If the medical needs involved only routine monitoring and preventive care, the person could remain in his/her own home and just receive services from physician offices and clinics. A more medically compromised elderly person would need the oversight that could be provided by a personal care home that could attend to daily living needs and make sure that the patient got seen by a doctor or nurse when needed. If the elderly person required 24-hour monitoring, medication and treatment by a registered nurse, a skilled nursing home would be the only appropriate setting. An acute medical crisis would require treatment in an acute hospital on a medical floor or in an intensive-care unit. Thus, the long term care consumer is processed up and down through this "continuum" from low intensity and complexity settings to high ones.

Organizing care along such a continuum produces a lot of problems. There is often little coordination among these different components. Records get lost and tests duplicated. In addition, since the needs of the elderly are constantly changing, lags in transfer mean that residents will be without needed services and may be exposed to unnecessary risks.

Moreover, the ill effects of transferring a frail elderly person from one setting to another, called "transfer trauma," can kill them. Some research
suggests that death rates rise in the first few months after a person is transferred to a nursing home (Thorson, 1988). One study noted an increase in
fall rates of residents after relocation to a new facility (Friedman, 1995).
Other studies have noted that patients suffering from dementia are more
seriously affected by relocation (Bredin, 1995; Robertson, 1995).

In contrast, as noted in Fig. 7.1, the Klaassen assisted-living model
organizes services so that they come to the consumer. Medical services are
coordinated by the facility and assistance with the tasks of daily living
(dressing, bathing, feeding, etc.) adjust to the needs of the resident.

The basic idea was not new, but the way it was packaged was brilliant. Indeed, about half of the long term care in the United States is
provided in this way informally by relatives and friends in the person's
home. Commercial and cooperative apartment complexes similarly
adapt, providing services as residents age and create "Naturally
Occurring Retirement Communities" or NORCs (Smith, 2003). Indeed,
those with enough money have always and will continue to receive care
in this way in their own home, hiring attendants, nurses and doctors as
needed. Rose Kennedy and Ronald Reagan, during their slow declines,
received all of their care at home in this way. Medicare and Medicaid
pay for hospice care so, at the very end, everyone can afford a similar option. It costs less and many people prefer to die in familiar
surroundings.

What was new was that Klaassen specifically designed new facilities
or "communities" with this purpose in mind. Sunrise and other developers responded perfectly to a growing market of adult children facing the
difficulties of caring for their aging parents. The ideological trappings surrounding these new communities served as a great sales pitch. There were
three basic elements to the pitch:

- *Home*: This is <u>not</u> a nursing home. Your apartment is your home. You
  furnish it and you are entitled to the same privacy and autonomy you
  would have in your own home.
- *Choice:* You and your children choose what services you will
  purchase. You are in charge.

- *Aging in Place:* The assisted living community, within broad limits, will provide whatever services you wish on site including medical, nursing and hospice services. Other than for brief periods of treatment and procedures in an acute-care hospital, you need never move again.

Many demographic trends helped stimulate the demand for such assisted-living developments.

- The 85 and older population was growing faster than any other segment and was projected to continue to grow at this pace.
- The supply of nursing home beds was not increasing. As a result of the growth in the elderly population, access was declining.
- The overall stock of nursing homes in the U.S., most constructed shortly after the passage of the Medicare and Medicaid legislation and before the reimbursement of construction costs were curtailed, was aging and many would soon reach the end of their useful life.
- The informal care long provided by adult children was disappearing. Adult children were increasingly geographically separated from their parents and increasingly living in two wage households.
- While in 1966, at the time of the implementation of the Medicare and Medicaid program, 28.5% of the elderly lived below poverty as compared to 14.7% of the population as a whole, by 2004, the elderly poverty rate had dropped to 9.8% as compared to 12.7% for the population as a whole (National Center for Health Statistics, 2007, Figure 4, pp. 93). During this period, strong lifetime earnings, good retirement benefits and Medicare had helped transform the elderly from the poorest age segment to the most affluent. At least one third could now afford the out-of-pocket costs of private assisted living.
- Changes in Medicare and Medicaid reimbursement incentives were beginning to transform the health system and nursing homes. Hospitals were pushing people out the door more quickly. Nursing homes no longer had any financial incentive to keep residents that did not require a lot of medical and nursing interventions. In the process, nursing homes were becoming less attractive places to live and to visit and the demand for an alternative for elderly persons with less complex medical needs was growing. The fees that private patients

had to pay for nursing home care were also rising. This made it easier to provide care for private pay patients in a more attractive and less costly alternative setting.

- For investors, assisted-living development was becoming the hot stock option. Real estate was seen as a pretty risk-free investment and developers claimed that, once a facility reached full occupancy, an investor could get more than a 30% return on their money.

Paul Klaassen and the Emergence of Sunrise Senior Living

Paul Klaassen's story bridges the older generation of "ma and pa" operated boarding homes and the newer generation of more aggressive developers. The Klaassens' decision to operate a facility, as it had been for many others, was in part motivated by their own experiences in getting assistance for elderly relatives in grim and impersonal nursing homes.

In 1981, the Klaassens sold their home and moved into a boarded up nursing home in northern Virginia. They bought and converted two other nursing homes and then in 1987, built their first prototype facility from scratch. It had a Victorian mansion style, capturing the flavor of an earlier era and became the trademark for their company, Sunrise Senior Living.

Klaassen became a key leader in the assisted-living movement, helping to found a new trade association, the Assisted Living Federation of America (ALFA). Five years later, a diverse industry that had previously lacked a name claimed revenues of almost $30 billion dollars and more than 30,000 facilities. Assisted-living had also become the darling of Wall Street investors. They were sold on the healthy returns that were promised and the perception of the safety of real estate investments.

The new industry was inundated with capital for expansion. Sunrise Senior Living, Inc., in its initial public offering in 1996 announced plans to open fifty-five new assisted-living facilities (which Sunrise referred to as "communities") by the end of 1999. This and a later offering raised $195 million dollars. "Compassion Pays" read the headline of the *Forbes* profile on Klaassen and the Sunrise operation (Forbes, 1997).

One community that was typical of the new communities that were built by Sunrise illustrates the thought and care that went into the site selection and design. It was located in an affluent suburb in a major east coast metropolitan area. The site was selected by Sunrise because it had a large number of households with heads aged 45–60 and incomes of more than $75,000 (These are the adult children likely to have aging parents who will relocate to be near them and who are likely to be able to afford its rates). Taking advantage of its ambiguous status, Sunrise was approved for construction as a senior apartment complex and not as a health facility. This avoided a lot of licensure and regulatory requirements that would have slowed construction and forced Sunrise to compromise the way it intended to operate. All the direct health and personal care services are provided by a licensed home health agency owned by Sunrise and operated within the facility.

The adult children are the facilities' "real" customers. About 50% of the square footage is devoted to attractive common areas in an attempt to encourage socialization. It also provides a favorable impression to adult children exploring options for their aging parents and helps assuage any guilt they may feel about institutionalizing their parent. Every detail is important in this facility. The wide porches and the large, little used, circular staircase in the center entrance give the impression of a wealthy Victorian mansion. It suggests that the new residents were being socially promoted rather than suffering the shameful stigma of being admitted to a nursing home, which many elderly view as equivalent to commitment to a poorhouse. An elegant Irish setter, the facility's mascot, greets those that enter. All of the thought that went into site selection, design and details were a success. The facility was filled in less than 100 days, almost three months ahead of schedule and continues to operate at over 95% occupancy. Almost half the residents have returned from Florida or other retirement resort locations to be closer to their children.

The facility takes the Sunrise vision of "aging in place" seriously. It will keep anyone except those that are medically unstable or who require IVs, tubes or vents. It provides care for incontinence and cognitive impairment that many other residential facilities for the elderly are unable to provide. Residents can make arrangements to receive hospice services.

The financing of care is all private pay and straightforward. If the residents run out of money, they are discharged. The facility does not ask for financial information before admitting residents. The financial condition of the applicant, however, is read in the body language of the adult children when the payment arrangements are explained. It is an informal process, but sufficient to assure that most residents have enough resources to sustain the costs incurred as a resident of the facility. Usually one of the adult children is the responsible party and signs the contract between the prospective resident and the managing company. In 2001, Sunrise Suburban was charging between $2,500 and $5,000 a month for a resident's apartment, meals and activities. Anything else was extra and the costs could add up. Personal care packages ranged from $23 a day to $65 a day, depending on the number of hours of personal care required. Administration of medication cost $8 a day for two administrations. Some residents expressed irritation about everything costing extra. One resident was annoyed to receive a large bill when all she needed was transportation to a doctor and help with dressing for two days. For residents with substantial personal care needs, the extra costs could amount to more than $50,000 a year.

Among the staff, there is none of the specialization typically seen in a hospital. Workers are expected to function universally and have broad job descriptions that include all of the tasks similar to those done by a mother for her child. There is a conscious attempt *not* to recruit individuals with experience working in nursing homes or other health-related settings. "Give me a lump of clay with a heart that I can mold rather than a nursing home aide," the director says. According to an administrator, the company looks for people who want a second family, and try to make the job fun, even though most of the jobs pay little above minimum wage. With this frugal approach to staffing and full occupancy, this facility has more than met the company's expectations for profitability.

Sunrise was the beneficiary of a seemingly un-ending supply of capital flowing from venture capital firms, stock offerings, and bank mortgages, joint ventures with local investors, sale and long term lease backs and management contracts with less experienced owners. In 2000, the entire Sunrise empire was valued at $1.1 billion and operated 148 facilities in 23 states and the United Kingdom that included a total capacity for 5,621 elderly residents.

Thus Klaassen was doing exactly what entrepreneurs and the resulting process of "creative destruction" of free markets are supposed to do — provide better combined products that cost less. He had created a real "killer application."

Discussion

- The case outlines the problems inherent in the "continuum of care" in the traditional medical model of providing care for the frail elderly. Does the assisted-living model really work better as its advocates in the case claim? Where are its major potential vulnerabilities?
- "The Sunrise assisted living model of creative destruction involved skimming the cream (private pay, easy care residents) away from the nursing homes sector weakening their financial viability and increasing the economic divisions in the long term care people receive. Is there a way to avoid this outcome and assure greater equity in care?"

Postscript

How well has Sunrise as a business proposition and as a model for the provision of services to the elderly borne the test of time?

There is no question that Sunrise has helped produce significant shifts in patterns of use in the United States. Overall use by the elderly of nursing homes has declined slightly over the last two decades, as has the proportion of private pay patients. The purpose of private assisted-living is to ensure that the more financially secure get care in a more homelike and less institutional setting, which in turn has exacerbated the income-related segregation of care. The less financially secure are relegated to nursing homes that may be more like the poor houses of the 19th century.

The recent scandals over quality of care have been more concentrated in the Sunrises and the other newer private assisted-living facilities rather than traditional nursing homes. Headlines about quality of care scandals now stigmatize assisted-living in the way nursing homes were stigmatized more than two decades ago. In 1999, a GAO report noted the lack of adequate consumer protections and major quality of care problems in the rapidly expanding assisted-living industry (Allen, 2008). Front page newspaper articles have highlighted in grim detail some of the problems (Goldstein, 2001; Fallis, 2004; USA Today, 2004; Dilanian and Phillips, 2007). An 82-year old woman suffocated with her head caught between her mattress and the side rails meant to keep her from falling out of bed in a private assisted-living facility outside of Detroit, complete with fireplaces and gleaming chandeliers

(Goldstein, 2001). The state attorney general filed charges against the company for involuntary manslaughter. A resident in a private facility in an affluent suburb outside of Philadelphia died of neglect resulting from repeated head wounds from falls. The facility took no steps to prevent these falls. The facility settled the subsequent lawsuit brought by the family for $525,000 (Dilanian and Phillips, 2007). Two incapacitated residents were neglected for hours, despite repeated calls for help and got assistance only by dialing 911 and summoning the police to a Sunrise Senior Living Facility in Alexandria, Virginia. The only care worker on duty had fallen asleep and was later convicted of neglect and sentenced to 180 days in jail. These upscale private pay facilities share many of the same quality of care problems that have long plagued the indigent boarding homes. They also share the same lack of adequate state regulatory oversight. Most credit the decline in such stories about nursing homes to the federal strengthening of inspection standards and the public reporting of results. Some consumer advocates argue for the need for similar standards in assisted-living, but the industry itself is resistant.

In addition, much of the assisted-living industry's pitch about its "new" model of care has proved illusory. Some developers initially claimed that the government had no more business regulating private-pay assisted-living than it did in regulating the care one chooses to pay for privately in one's own home. Yet, an assisted-living facility is not a home. Residents typically sign an agreement upon admission acknowledging that they do not have the rights of a tenant as provided for by state law and that the facility can discharge a resident at any time it chooses. These agreements are reasonable since the facility must be able to assure the safety of residents. Residents, as a result, are not afforded the same rights that a tenant has in a private apartment. Indeed, state legislation subsequently used such agreements as a way of defining assisted-living facilities that must meet state licensure standards. The Sunrise facility described in this case must now comply with these licensure requirements. The choices residents have are not the same as those they would have in their own home. They do not own the facility as many own their own home. The real owners buy and sell these facilities, using the occupants as assets, often quite rapidly without involving residents in these choices. The idea of a "risk contract" that would protect the facility from lawsuits, but permit residents to take risks (e.g. taking walks unattended, being a diabetic and choosing an inappropriate diet, etc), has been suggested by the Assisted Living Federation of America but does not seem to have been put in practice in many facilities. Finally, only a few assisted-living companies, such as Sunrise, have attempted to provide for aging in place. Even in Sunrise, such arrangements fall short of what it would be possible to provide in one's own home. It is perhaps impossible for licensed facilities designed to provide a certain standard of care to be completely flexible in meeting the individual needs of a resident. While one can organize services for an individual to age in place in their own home, it becomes more problematic for a licensed facility. As the residents of a licensed assisted-living facility age in place together, they cross a threshold and it becomes an unlicensed nursing home.

Since 2000, Sunrise Senior Services continued to grow, initially managing to avoid some of the accumulating difficulties faced by other national private assisted-living chains. Sunrise, through its construction of new facilities, acquisition of other chains, and management contracts expanded from 148 facilities in 2000 to an empire of more than 459 in 2008 and from a resident capacity of 5,621 in 2000 to 39,214 during this same period (Assisted Living Executive, 2008). This represented a more than six fold increase in resident capacity in eight years. Total assets increased to more than $1.7 billion. Sunrise had become by far the largest assisted-living chain in the nation.

In the last two years, however, the problems at Sunrise have grown and expansion has ground to halt. Net income declined from $83 million in 2005 to a loss of $70 million in 2007 and the losses in 2008 were substantially larger. As the overall real estate and financial markets have ground to a halt, Sunrise has had to write off construction projects it was in the process of completing. It is no longer involved in the construction of any new facilities. It also suffered a serious financial blow when a real estate investment trust, Health Care REIT, backed out of a $643.5 million deal to acquire a 90% stake in 29 of its facilities. Sunrise would have realized at least $41 million from the deal (Pristin, 2008). The same external real estate and financial market forces that fueled its expansion are now fueling its contraction.

These external market problems have been exacerbated by an accumulating list of internal ones. In 2006, the Klaassens sold stock shares worth $20 million shortly before the company announced accounting problems that had overstated previous earnings, and precipitated a plunge in the stock. The Chief Financial Officer, fired as a result of these disclosures, has since sued the company for breach of contract, claiming that he was fired in retaliation for his disclosure of improper and in some cases fraudulent accounting practices to the SEC. The Service Employees International Union, an institutional investor of pension funds in Sunrise, demanded an independent investigation of what it suspected to be insider trading (Pristin, 2008). In November 2008, Sunrise was in violation of certain covenants imposed by its lenders. Stock prices, which had been trading at a value as high as 40 dollars a share in 2007, dropped to 27 cents a share in November 2008. In that same month, Paul Klaassen, founder and Chief Executive Officer of Sunrise for 27 years and the embodiment of the vision of a new way of organizing care for the elderly, stepped down. The revised financial statements for 2008 released in March 2009 showed Sunrise on shaky financial footing. It continues to negotiate with lenders for terms that will prevent it from being forced into bankruptcy (Lazo, 2009). In the midst of the larger real estate and financial storm, Sunrise itself may be a victim of creative destruction.

Discussion

- The problem with institutional regulation is that it limits the degree of flexibility one can have in addressing the individual needs of residents and thus does not permit aging in place. How could this be overcome?
- Other forms of ownership in which the residents and their families really own the facility rather than stock holders and private investors (e.g. coops condominium, etc) could possibly assure more viability to the ideals of the assisted-living movement. Would it work?

8

Diagnosing and Treating the Pathologies of the U.S. Health System

> *So oft in theologic wars,*
> *The disputants, I ween,*
> *Rail on in utter ignorance*
> *Of what each other mean,*
> *And prate about an Elephant*
> *Not one of them has seen*
>
> *(Saxe, 1970)*

Recurring Themes

Like the blind men and the elephant, we grasp at different solutions to the pathologies described by the cases in this book. If nothing else, these cases illustrate how complex the organization and financing of healthcare is and how unpredictable the results can be. The prevailing assumptions and ideologies at any point in time soon get stood on their head. Risk-based total capitation contracts with integrated delivery systems, once assumed to be the inevitable wave of the future, have given way to provider approaches to contracting that are more fragmented, as well as a selective service line approach.

Our diagnosis of the pathologies depends on where we are standing. Physicians and other health-related professions argue that healthcare is a professional, altruistic service that the nation should nurture and support. Businesses that purchase healthcare for their employees see it as another cost that they have to absorb that has to be managed more efficiently. The average patient and his or her family are preoccupied with the need for a trusting relationship in a fragmented system frayed beyond the breaking point. Yet, all of these perspectives and the stories in this book suggest that profound and unpredictable changes loom.

This chapter focuses on the efforts to treat the health system's diverse pathologies. Case 14 provides the story about the difficulties of a local hospital "conversion" foundation in promoting health in a community with growing social and economic divisions. Conversion foundations are set up to hold the assets from the sale of a non-profit to a for-profit to continue its original mission. Just not having to function as a business, however, did not solve the problem of translating a mission into an agenda with dollars attached to it. Case 15 describes the efforts to address the cost, quality and access problems through healthcare reform at a state level and its implications for bridging the ideological divide at the national level. The Obama administration now has the challenge of forging a treatment plan among groups clinging to very different parts of the elephant.

Case 14: Pottstown Hospital's Conversion Foundation[14]

Background

> *The school auditorium was packed. The audience listened impa-*
> *tiently as an epidemiologist from the state health department went*
> *through the cancer registry numbers for the town's zip code. There*
> *was little difference in the incident rates for the Pottstown area and*
> *those of the state as a whole. The audience did not want to hear this*
> *and many had already lined up along the wall of the auditorium wait-*
> *ing for a turn to speak. A young blond woman spoke first, her voice*

---

[14] The author assisted in the needs assessment conducted for the Pottstown Area Health and Wellness Foundation and this account is based on that report and is also indebted to insights of many of the area's residents who were interviewed in the process of completing that report and to John Harris and other DGA Partners participants that assisted with this effort.

and hands trembling, "I want you to look at this picture; this was
my three year old son. He died of a brain tumor. The doctors said
it was due to 'environmental factors.' I'll never hear his voice or
hold him in my arms, due to those 'environmental factors' in the
landfill!"

On the surface, there seemed nothing about Pottstown that would create the concerns that packed the school auditorium. The houses in most of
its neighborhoods are well maintained on attractive streets in a town nes-
tled along the Schuylkill River. Pottstown seemed an idyllic center in one
of the most rapidly growing parts of the Philadelphia metropolitan area. It
is filled with historic pre-revolutionary buildings and well maintained
churches. Perched in its center is the attractive campus of the Hill School,
an elite private boarding school. Pottstown boasts the most professional
orchestra in the region outside the City of Philadelphia and a growing art
scene. Two other older factory towns along the Schuylkill, but closer to
Philadelphia, have recently gone through remarkable revitalizations as
residential areas, watering holes and upper scale shopping centers for
young urban professionals. Clearly, Pottstown was next.

However, for the angry school auditorium audience, problems had
been simmering for a long time. The immediate concern prompting the
meeting was the landfill on the edge of their town. From the perspective
of Pottstown residents, their neighbors in the small township of West
Pottsgrove had made a pact with the Devil, Waste Management Inc.,
swapping the use of 300 acres for the money that freed residents from
paying any local real estate taxes for the municipality or for its schools.
Pottstown residents whose houses bordered on the edge of the dump
complained of noxious fumes and a troubling number of family members and neighbors who were suffering or had died from cancer. As
many as 350 trucks a day dumped at the site which had grown seven-
fold in size in the last twenty years. There was not much control or
record keeping of what had ended up in the landfill over its more than
fifty year history but it had received waste from all over the east coast
and as far away as Canada. The landfill was now running out of space
and Waste Management had recently applied for a 40 acre "vertical expansion" (Stahl, 2003). The proposed expansion raised Federal Aviation

Administration (FAA) safety concerns about the local airport that also borders the site.

For long time residents of Pottstown, the dump was just the last of a long history of assaults on their town. Pottstown had served as the center of the iron and steel industry for two hundred years. It had become a thriving boom town in the early 20th century, but went into a long and painful decline beginning in the 1960's. The Firestone Rubber plant closed in 1969 followed by the Bethlehem Steel mills in 1971. More than 3,000 workers lost their jobs. Since then, Pottstown has faced an accumulating series of environmental concerns that had made residents distrustful and hostile to the increasingly remote forces that were shaping and, possibly, shortening their lives. Waste Management Inc., the "top of the heap" in waste disposal, is a multinational Fortune 500 company based in Houston, Texas, that had more than $13 billion in revenues in 2007. Waste Management occupied just one corner of a "toxic triangle," as described by some residents. On the second corner was the Limerick Nuclear Reactor whose towers and steam vapors are clearly visible in the town. The Limerick Nuclear reactor is owned by the Excelon Corporation, the nation's largest producer of electricity, based in Chicago, Illinois, with about $19 billion in revenues a year. The third corner, at the edge of Pottstown on the Schuylkill River, was occupied by a plant of Occidental Chemical, a subsidiary of Occidental. The multi-national oil, gas and chemical conglomerate based in Los Angeles, had $18.7 billion in sales in 2007. Occidental Chemical is the nation's largest producer of poly vinyl chloride (PVC). A by-product of the production of PVC is Dioxin which has been linked to cancer. If this were not enough to add to the suspicions of Pottstown residents, Occidental Chemical had purchased Hooker Chemical in 1968. One of Hooker Chemical's previous sites, Love Canal in Niagara Falls, was used for a long time as a dumping site for toxic chemicals. This canal was later filled in and used as the site for a school and a residential development. The high incidence of cancer and birth defects on the Love Canal site eventually received national attention. Residents were relocated and Occidental paid $128 million in restitution to them. "Quite simply," the regional Environmental Protection Agency administrator at the time observed, "Love Canal is one of the most appalling environmental tragedies in American history... What is worse is that it cannot be regarded as an isolated event. It could happen again— anywhere in this country." (Beck, 1979). Perhaps it was happening in Pottstown.

While this "toxic triangle," governed by distant, powerful corporate conglomerates fed the suspicions of long time Pottstown residents, their concerns about being a dumping ground did not stop with toxic biochemical waste. Many residents felt that Pottstown had also become a dumping ground for people as well. Montgomery County is the second most affluent county and the one with the highest housing costs in Pennsylvania. However, there was a growing, "deinstitutionalized" psychiatric, mentally handicapped and substance abuse population that needed community-based living arrangements. Pottstown was one of the few places in the county with housing prices that would fit the budgets of the agencies responsible for their care. It was also perhaps too disorganized and demoralized to mount an effective "Not in my backyard" (NIMBY) campaign to prevent the purchase and rental of housing for this purpose. Many of the long time residents of Pottstown were frightened by these newcomers that often seemed to be wandering aimlessly in the downtown business district. They believed that this was making it impossible to revitalize the downtown and attract the businesses and homebuyers desperately needed to prevent further decline of the town's tax base.

In the midst of all this, an anguished struggle took place over the future of their hospital, Pottstown Memorial. A critical juncture for the hospital came in 1998 with the recognition of the need to expand its emergency room and modernize its physical plant. Pottstown Memorial, created out of a merger of two older existing hospitals, was constructed in the 1970s. The local industries that had helped support the fund drive for the hospital now no longer existed. The consultant hired to assess the feasibility of a fund drive to pay for the expansion and renovation concluded that such a fund drive was unrealistic, given the current economic make up of the town. The money for the expansion could have been borrowed, but this seemed risky. Future trends in hospital reimbursement did not look promising. Some of the hospital's board members had struggled as executives of Pottstown's dying industries and had been chastened by that experience. They did not want to be responsible for the closing of the town's hospital, now its largest remaining employer. How can we, they thought, assure the long term future of the hospital? Clearly, free-standing hospitals were going to have a difficult time. After considerable negotiations and assurances of the desired capital investments and an acceptable level of indigent care, the hospital was sold to Community Health Systems, a for-profit community hospital chain based in Brentwood, Tennessee.

The sale would provide more than $65 million for a "conversion foundation" and they would need to go to the judge of Orphan's Court in Montgomery County to get approval for the plan. (HealthEast in the first case in this book had run afoul of the judge of Orphan's Court in Allentown, similarly responsible for the oversight of local charities). The Pottstown Area Health and Wellness Foundation, as it was named, would honor the charitable mission of those that had contributed to the hospital over the years. However, only with the completion of the sale did discussion begin about how this money should be used. The purpose, as its name proclaimed, was to improve the health and wellness of those that had been served by the hospital, but how? One could use the funds to address the needs of the not particularly welcome deinstitutionalized newcomers. Alternatively, one could focus on the concerns of the local environmental activists which some of the hospital's board thought were a little crazy. Most of the members of the fledgling foundation were former board members of the hospital and many liked the safer idea of using the funds to promote healthy behavior (e.g. smoking cessation, exercise, weight reduction, etc.). From the perspective of many long time residents of Pottstown, this was "blaming the victim" and they used angry and unprintable language to describe it. The Foundation board knew they were in a minefield and they wanted to tread it carefully and only after careful study.

The Pottstown Area Health Assessment (Smith, 2004)

The health problems of the Borough of Pottstown in 2004 stood out in stark contrast to the rest of Pottstown Memorial Hospital's service area. While the rest of the service area had disease specific age-adjusted death rates that for the most part, were substantially below the same rates for Pennsylvania and the nation as a whole, the Pottstown rates were substantially higher. In contrast to the rest of the hospital's service area, Pottstown's total age-adjusted death rate was 31% higher than for the rest of the region and almost 60% higher for chronic lower respiratory disease and diabetes. The death rates from accidents were 71% higher than for the rest of the region. We all die, so perhaps a more relevant measure of the quality of life are the potential years of life lost per 1,000 people under the age of 65. Here again, on this measure of lost life, the Borough of Pottstown was substantially above overall Pennsylvania and national rates and the rest of the Pottstown service area was substantially below. The Borough of Pottstown's years of potential life lost per 1,000 under the age of 65 was more than twice as high as that of the rest of the service area (65.6 vs. 31.0). In terms of health survey information, Pottstown residents were more likely to report their health as fair or poor, being a victim of violent crime or domestic violence, more likely to report chronic lung disease including bronchitis or emphysema, major depression, and migraine or severe headaches.

What accounted for these substantial differences? Lots of things.

The environmental and industrial history of Pottstown Borough may have contributed. Concerns about the "toxic triangle" and resulting illnesses were the most frequently mentioned health concern of residents in the area surveyed.

More general social and economic determinants also certainly played a role. In contrast to most of the other townships whose populations increased dramatically between the 1990 and 2000 census, the population of Pottstown Borough declined. Pottstown Borough also had the lowest median family income of any of the township in the service area, the lowest proportion of people over 25 with a college degree, the second highest unemployment rate, the highest percent of families in poverty, and by far the highest crime rate.

Access to health services no doubt contributed to these differences. Pottstown Borough residents reported more difficulty getting to see a physician and were more likely to report that the cost of physician care and the cost of prescription medications caused them to avoid seeking care they felt they needed. Yet, surprisingly, those below 200% of poverty were more likely to report receiving the recommended screening and prevention services. This perhaps reflects the concerted efforts of public health officials to target the low income population for screening and lack of a convenient source of care for the more recently arrived residents in the growing suburban parts of Pottstown Hospital's service area.

Yet, the behavior of Pottstown Borough residents certainly also played a role in their poor health. Borough resident smoking rates were significantly higher as were rates of binge and chronic drinking. Borough residents were also more likely to be obese and less likely to engage in vigorous exercise. Almost twice as many children between the ages of six and 17 were reported to be overweight (30.7%).

Service providers and residents alike echoed two recurring themes. The first was, "this is a real community." They emphasized that people take care of each other, know each other and extended families stick together and live close to each other. Perhaps reflecting this and in spite of the generally poor health statistics, there was virtually no difference in infant mortality rates between the Borough of Pottstown and the rest of the service area. The other theme was, "we do a lot with a little." They were proud of what they were able to do with very little money. For example, a successful meals-on-wheels program for the home-bound elderly had been cobbled together with donations and volunteers at a fraction of what such programs typically cost.

The board of the Pottstown Health and Wellness Foundation was left to ponder over these health statistics for their service area and what they meant for how they should use the funds from the hospital sale.

Discussion

- What is really happening to produce the health differences between the Borough of Pottstown and the rest of the service area?
- What should the Pottstown Health and Wellness Foundation do to best accomplish its mission?

Postscript

In the five years since its establishment, the Pottstown Health and Wellness Foundation has become a familiar and active participant in the local scene. It has moved to new headquarters on the fifth floor of an old bank building at the center of the Borough of Pottstown and is an important component of its redevelopment efforts. Its new headquarters have a commanding view of the region it serves. The foundation drew up a long range strategic plan based on the needs assessment. In its grant making, it has straddled the conflicting sensitivities of its community, judiciously maintaining the four goals agreed upon at the outset in that strategic plan (Pottstown Health and Wellness Foundation, 2009). Those goals were:

1. Reduce Behavioral Risks:

- Empower individuals to make healthier lifestyle choices by providing information, programs, and support in several areas, including diet and exercise; drug and alcohol; mental/spiritual health and stress management.
- Reduce behavioral risks from prenatal through high school by sponsoring health education programs for children and their parents.
- Build on social networks of religious and other community organizations to support outreach programs related to health and wellness with particular interest in healthy lifestyles.

2. Improve Access to Medical Services:

- Improve access to health services by providing information to support seamless access to care.
- Strengthen existing agencies involved in distributing healthcare and disease prevention information.
- Support Pottstown's health center, Community Health & Dental Care, especially with regard to its education and prevention programs.
- Improve access to preventive services including screenings and vaccines.
- Improve access to health services by enhancing transportation or convenience of the services.

3. Enhance Formal and Informal Supports:

- Support the infrastructure needs and organizational effectiveness of key community not-for-profit organizations that provide preventive health programs.

4. Improve Physical and Social Environment:

- Encourage physical activities in the region by improving the recreational infrastructure.
- Support efforts to improve environmental health conditions caused by local pollution sources.
- Reinforce the social strength and mutual support of family units and caregivers to address issues such as distressed teens, care for the elderly, chronically ill and homebound, domestic violence and encourage an atmosphere of individual safety and non-violence.

By the end of fiscal year 2008, the Pottstown Health and Wellness Foundation had invested in the accomplishment of all of these goals. It had given out a total $9.6 million in the form of 245 separate grants, with the largest pieces of the pie going for efforts to reduce behavioral risks ($3.56 million) and to improve access to medical services ($2.56) million. The third and fourth priorities, enhance formal and informal supports and improve the physical and social environment, received $1.75 million each (Pottstown Health and Wellness Foundation, 2008). The Foundation had provided more than a million dollars in support of the development of a new community health and dental center. It opened its doors in November 2008 and cares for Pottstown's growing population of uninsured. It has also provided support for temporary housing and a food kitchen for the poor. The clinic and other services, it should be noted, were sited on the periphery of the town, adjacent to its airport and well away from the downtown business district. The Foundation has focused mostly on upbeat and feel good projects, perhaps consciously trying to counter the pervasive pessimism and suspicion, side-effects of Pottstown's long decline.

The local environmental activist concerns about the "toxic triangle" in the meantime have been partly mollified. The Secretary of the Department of Environmental Protection, appointed by the newly elected Democratic Governor, Ed Rendell, announced at a press conference at the site with other local officials in December 2003 that the Pottstown Landfill would not be awarded an expansion and would be closed. The legal battle and the concerns about the costs of assuring the safety of the capped landfill continued for another five years. In August 2008, the Borough of Pottstown signed a contract with Waste Management to assist in the treatment of the leachate or poisoning of the ground water from the landfill for $500,000. The Occidental Chemical plant closed shortly after the landfill in 2005, producing a loss of about 200 jobs. "Hey, Oxy has plenty of plants in Texas, and they are going to go where they're wanted," said the Pottstown Area Chamber of Commerce Director, who had tried to keep the company in Pottstown (Brandt, 2005). The national and increasingly global debate over the tradeoff between jobs and environmental quality continues in Pottstown. With the closing of Oxy, much of that debate, however, has shifted to who pays for the clean up of the toxic wastes left previously by Firestone and then by Occidental on the site. The 257 acre property is located along the Schuylkill River in the middle of a planned scenic trail along the river that would extend into the City of Philadelphia. However, the issues related to the cleanup of the site must be addressed before any plans for converting it to recreational use can go ahead.

Pottstown Memorial Hospital under Community Health Systems management has enjoyed three years of growing financial health (PHC4, 2009). While revenues have grown at an average of 11% a year, expenses have grown only 7% per year. The hospital had an operating margin of 14% in Fiscal Year 2007 which translated into a net income of 12.3 million dollars. Two percent of the care it provided was uncompensated, about average for suburban hospitals in the region, and 13% of its care was for Medicaid patients, higher than all but two of the twenty-two hospitals in the Philadelphia area's suburban counties.

While the financial downturn that began in 2008 may pose new challenges, the health and wellness of Pottstown Memorial Hospital's service area appears to be on the mend.

Discussion

- How well have the funding allocations of the Pottstown Health and Wellness Foundation responded to the needs reflected in the assessment?

- Monday morning quarterbacking is never fair, but we do it anyway. The operating margin of the hospital in the 2007 fiscal year was $12.3 million, while total Foundation funding allocation since its inception resulting from the sale of the hospital to Community Health Systems totaled $9.6 million. Most of the operating margin of the hospital, had it not been sold, could possibly have been used to cover similar programs and services. As Case 1 (HealthEast) illustrated, however, it is more likely that these surpluses would have been put to use in the pursuit of competitive advantage in a medical arms race. The hospital, now for-profit, helps to support the Borough of Pottstown with taxes. Did the hospital board make the right decision in selling Pottstown's hospital?

Case 15: State and Federal Healthcare Reform Initiatives: From Rendell to Obama[15]

Background

States have always served as an incubator for federal legislation and programs. For example, the original Social Security legislation signed into law by President Roosevelt in 1935 reflected earlier legislation in New York and other states. After the failed passage of the health insurance legislation sponsored by the Clinton Administration in 1993, prospects for such legislation at the federal level dimmed over the next decade. State

---

[15] The author served on an advisory panel to the Governor's Office of Health Care Reform and some of this case is based on these discussions and the miscellaneous research and policy distillations developed for the Office. In addition, it also makes use of a previously published analysis of the Democratic and Republican Presidential candidate healthcare reform proposals by Andrulis, D., D. B. Smith *et al.* (2008). Health Care Proposals of the 2008 Democratic and Republican Presidential Nominees: Implications for Improving Access, Affordability and Quality for America's Minorities. Washington D.C., The Joint Center on Economic and Political Studies.

initiatives became the only game in town. Edward Rendell became governor of Pennsylvania in a landslide victory in 2003. He was anxious to get in on the action. His first act as governor was to create the Governor's Office of Health Care Reform. Reflecting his earlier frenetic activity as Mayor of Philadelphia, Rendell assigned the office a complex and ambitious agenda. He appointed Rosemarie Greco, a prominent bank executive in Philadelphia, as director of the office. What Greco lacked in background in healthcare she made up in both commitment to the cause of healthcare reform and political skill in negotiating with potential adversaries. The $48,000 token salary she received in this position was symbolic of her commitment. The threat of the growing number of uninsured among the employed population in Pennsylvania was only one piece of the puzzle that needed to be solved. Improving the actual quality of care, addressing the healthcare work force needs and, most importantly, reducing cost increases for care, were essential, interrelated pieces. Healthcare reform required a multipronged approach.

The goal of the Governor's Office of Health Care Reform was to coordinate executive branch efforts to develop a comprehensive plan to address the accessibility, affordability and the quality of healthcare in Pennsylvania. The Director of the Office for Health Care reform served as chairperson of the "Health Care Reform Cabinet," which included the Secretaries of the Department of Corrections, Aging, Health, Welfare and the Commissioner of Insurance. The basic weakness of state-based healthcare reform efforts are that they are limited by the national forces beyond their control that shape insurance coverage and the accessibility, affordability and quality of healthcare. States also typically have more difficulty obtaining the funding to support these efforts. The basic strengths of states in addressing healthcare reform, as the composition of Pennsylvania's "Health Care Reform Cabinet" suggests, is that they have the "boots on the ground" licensing, regulating, contracting with and overseeing the actions of insurance companies, employers, health professionals and institutional providers of care.

These strengths and weaknesses selectively affected the success of different parts of the agenda of the Office of Health Care Reform. A major challenge was that the new Governor lacked much traction in the legislature that was roughly evenly split between Democrats and Republicans in the House, while Republicans held a solid majority in the Senate. Faced with Republican members of the legislature with little interest in supporting the success of any of the new Democratic Governor's initiatives, the Office of Health Care Reform devoted much of its effort to finding and exploiting funding that did not require legislative appropriations to press their agenda forward.

One initial source of support, as for other states interested in exploring ways to expand insurance coverage, were federal Health Resources and Services Administration (HRSA) State Planning Grants. Pennsylvania's $900,000 grant enabled the hiring of an array of national consultants and the formation of a large and diverse state-wide advisory group including business leaders, healthcare professionals, provider associations, legislators and academics to guide the development of their strategic plan. A wide variety of reports were requested from Mathematica Policy Research Inc. and other national consulting firms, evaluating initiatives in other states to expand or retain employer based coverage and to control cost and improve quality. Four advisory panels met quarterly beginning in the fall of 2005: The Small Employers Panel, The Cost Containment of Health Care and Health Care Insurance Panel, The Quality in Health Care Panel and the Accessible, Cost-Effective Publicly Funded Health Care Panel. From all of these diverse efforts, a plan emerged, *Prescription Pennsylvania* that was released at a well attended briefing at the Governor's residence in Harrisburg on January 17, 2007.

Prescription Pennsylvania

"Prescription Pennsylvania" was described as "a set of integrated practical strategies for improving the healthcare of all Pennsylvanians, making the healthcare system more efficient and containing cost" (Governor's Office of Health Care Reform, 2007). It offered three prescriptions:

1. **RX for Affordability** focused on expanding health insurance by spreading the cost of such expanded coverage as evenly as possible. This included:
   a. Proposing a "Cover All Pennsylvanians" (CAP) plan to provide state subsidized private insurance to employers with 50 or fewer employees who earn less than the state average wage. The employer, the employee and the state were each responsible for

covering a portion of the cost. Families earning less than 300% of the Federal poverty level could also participate in the subsidized program no matter what the size of the company they worked for and no employer would get a "free ride" by opting out of providing coverage for their employees since those failing to provide coverage would be assessed a percentage of their payroll to support such coverage. In addition, in order to close another gap in health coverage, universities and colleges in the state would be required to phase in insurance coverage for students as a condition of admission and study.

b. The private insurance industry would be subjected to greater oversight, assuring a level playing field by requiring plans to provide a standardized basic package, controlling rate setting and assuring that at least 85% of premiums be used to pay for healthcare.

c. Providers of services would also face more rigorous accountability. Non-profit hospitals, in return for their tax exempt status, would be required to meet uniform "community benefit" standards in terms of expenditures for indigent care and other free services to their community. Providers would also receive more oversight to assure fair and standardized admissions and billing practices in order to ensure that some hospitals would not profit at the expense of others. More cost and quality information would be made available to assure informed consumer choices. In addition, the Office intended to establish a process that would ensure that large capital projects met regional healthcare needs and could be afforded by the payers in a region (i.e. a quasi Certificate of Need program, although the Office was careful not to use that term). Hospitals would also be required to develop emergency room screening and referral of non-emergency cases to a more appropriate and less costly level of care at the hospital.

2. **RX for Access** focused on addressing the workforce issues that tended to limit access to timely and appropriate care while adding to the cost of that care. This included:

a. Expanding the scope of practice of nurses, nurse practitioners, midwives, physician assistants, pharmacists and dental hygienists to allow them to practice to the fullest extent allowed by their education and training.

b. Assisting in providing startup resources in primary care shortage areas for the development of federally qualified health centers and nurse managed care centers and guidelines for insurers to use for appropriately compensating allied health providers.

c. Providing financial incentives to providers to support evening and weekend coverage and reduce the reliance on emergency departments.

d. Seeking ways to broaden the diversity of the healthcare workforce provide access to language services and culturally competent care in order to decrease healthcare disparities.

3. **RX for Quality** argued that improving the quality of care, enhancing patient safety and promoting wellness was also essential for reducing costs. This prescription proposed to:

a. Eliminate hospital-acquired infections, medical errors and unnecessary and ineffective care by ceasing to pay for care associated with these problems and requiring hospitals to adopt system-wide quality management and error reduction systems and interoperable electronic medical records.

b. Promote a pay-for-performance system led by the state and other major payers that reward quality of care.

c. Establish a payment system that encouraged effective chronic disease management for such conditions as heart disease, diabetes and asthma. These conditions currently involve costly and potentially avoidable hospitalizations that could be prevented with effective chronic disease management.

d. Prescription Pennsylvania also included an acknowledgment of the need to address the problems of long term care through: (1) more integrated care for those with substance abuse and mental disorders; (2) better palliative care and pain management and effective use of hospices in end of life care; (3) improving the quality of information related to long term care and delivering more services in home and community based settings and (4) assuring reliable long term care insurance products.

e. Finally, Prescription Pennsylvania focused on the wellness and healthy lifestyle problems that added to healthcare costs by (1) focusing on making all workplaces, restaurants and bars smoke-free and by implementing incentives to reward healthy behavior of consumers and (2) increasing wellness education and expanding access to school breakfasts and nutritious foods throughout the day in the state's public schools.

The devil, of course, would be in the details. Success of the agenda required shared sacrifices by providers, insurers, employers and the general public.

Discussion

- What are the advantages and disadvantages of such a multi-dimensional integrated plan for healthcare reform as opposed to just pursuing separate initiatives?
- Given the strengths and weaknesses described in the background section, what components of this agenda are going to be the easiest and the most difficult to accomplish?

Postscript

Prescription Pennsylvania, in the three years since its unveiling in January 2007, has met with mixed success. More than ten states during this same period began similar initiatives and only Massachusetts has had successes in substantially reducing the proportion of their population that is uninsured. The debate over healthcare reform again became a national one during the 2008 presidential campaign. The Obama transition team was interested in being debriefed about the lessons of the Pennsylvania experience. It had been a key swing state, critical to Obama's election success. It was, as a result, a litmus test for the prospects for national healthcare reform. The Pennsylvania litmus test provided the Obama Administration with both good and bad news.

The Good News

Prescription Pennsylvania showed that it was possible with incremental efforts to improve access and quality and, possibly, reduce long term costs. The Governor's plan made important progress with the second and third piece of the three components of its strategic plan, RX Access and RX Quality. This was accomplished through legislation, executive orders and public-private partnerships facilitated by the Office of Health Care Reform.

In July 2007, the Governor signed legislation expanding the scope of practice for nurse practitioners, nurse midwives, and dental hygienists. Pennsylvania had one of the most restrictive scopes of practice laws for these licensed professionals in the country. A nurse midwife could not even write a prescription for prenatal vitamins and dental hygienists could not care for patients in a nursing home without the simultaneous attendance of a dentist. Rosemarie Greco, Director of the Office of Health Care Reform, became involved in shuttle diplomacy between representatives of the nursing profession and the Pennsylvania Medical Society hammering out an agreement that eased passage of the legislation. The Governor's Office of Health care Reform saw this as a key piece of the puzzle in creating a lower cost, more coordinated team approach to care.

According to reports of the Pennsylvania Hospital Cost Containment Council, hospital-acquired infections in 2005 killed almost the same number who died in the twin towers 9/11 attack and contributed to additional hospital charges amounting to approximately $3.5 billion in Pennsylvania. The Governor signed into law Act 52 in July 2007 requiring infection surveillance procedures in hospitals and public reporting. The Hospital and Healthsystem Association of Pennsylvania supported the legislation. Pennsylvania can make a convincing case that it leads the nation in addressing the problem of hospital-acquired infections. According to preliminary findings released in January 2009, the combination of infection surveillance procedures and public reporting appears to have begun to have an effect in reducing incidence rates and deaths related to these infections (Pennsylvania Health Care Cost Containment Council, 2009).

Perhaps the most promising examples of the kinds of public private partnerships forged by state leadership in health reform embodied in the

Prescription Pennsylvania initiative was in chronic disease management. Approximately eighty percent of the costs of healthcare are incurred by the twenty percent of the population with one or more chronic conditions. Primary care physicians can potentially make the most difference in reducing the cost of chronic care and improving the outcomes. Yet, as illustrated in Case 9 (MDVIP), they are unrewarded by health plans for engaging in the necessary extra effort and are disengaging from such care. By executive order, the Governor appointed a commission in 2007 to make recommendations on how to address the problem. What emerged from its recommendations was a joint venture between the Governor's Office of Health Care Reform, private health insurance plans and a diverse collection of providers of primary care. They adopted a combination of the Chronic Care Model developed by Ed Wagner, head of a research institute at the Group Health Cooperative of Puget Sound (Wagner, Austin *et al.*, 1996) and the National Committee for Quality Assurance (NCQA) that supported the idea of a patient-centered medical home. The health insurance plans provided the financial support for the development, training and implementation of the model. Four hundred primary care practices, including academic health centers, nurse practitioner practices, federally qualified health centers, and small private physician practices are participating in four regional Learning Collaboratives. Together, these participating practices are responsible for the care of about 750,000 patients.

What makes the training, restructuring and delivery of these enriched services possible is the financial support of the health plans. With the Office of Health Care Reform convening the meetings that would have been impossible for the insurers to convene on their own without violating antitrust laws, financing arrangements were hammered out with all the major health plans participating. Medicare fee-for-service is the only major payer not participating. These plans, arch rivals in the market, share the costs of the project based on the proportion of their subscribers receiving care in the practice for a three year period. The Governor's Office of Health Care Reform covered the cost of training sessions for practice teams and the plans paid a sum to reimburse the lost revenue for attending the training sessions, cost of the patient registry, cost for clerical staff to do data entry into the registry and cost of applying for NCQA certification as a patient-centered medical home. Upon receiving

a Level 1 NCQA certification, the health insurers in the Southeast region —
the first collaborative to launch — agreed to provide an additional $28,000–
$40,000 a year for each full-time practitioner in a practice, depending on
the size of the practice, and up to $66,500–$95,000 per practitioner upon
reaching Level 3 certification.

While the evaluation of its effectiveness in improving the quality of
care and reducing the costs must wait, according to the Director of the
Office of Health Care Reform, the response of the participating physicians
has been enthusiastic. "This is the most exciting thing in my career,"
several have said. Another said, "I like the practice of medicine again."
Indeed, the Governor's Office of Health Care Reform is planning three more
Learning Collaboratives for about 100 additional practices because of the
interest shown by practices to participate in the training without payments
from the plans upon attaining NCQA certification (Torregrossa, 2009).

In March 2008, the Governor signed the executive order creating the
Pennsylvania Health Information Exchange. The goal is to assure state
wide interoperability of electronic health records by hospitals, laborato-
ries and pharmacies. The Obama Administration stimulus investment in
health information technology will expedite the accomplishment of these
goals. If the federal carrots are not sufficient to accomplish the conversion
of hospitals to electronic medical records, the stick, in terms of Medicare
and Medicaid penalties are planned to begin to kick in 2014.

Other parts of the strategic plan have been implemented. The law ban-
ning smoking in public places has been passed. A state website for com-
paring prescription prices at drug stores near to where consumers live is
in operation, taking advantage of information accumulated in the state
prescription program for low income seniors. The website is part of a
broader effort to provide greater market competition.

Other parts of the Prescription Pennsylvania initiative have been
slower to implement but have begun to take shape. A coordinated statewide strategic long term care plan designed in the long run to ease access
and reduce the overall costs, allowing people to age in place along the
lines described in Case 13 (Aging, Klaassen and the Killer Application)
has begun to take shape. A State of Maine-type approach to capping
regional capital expenditures in lieu of returning to a certificate of need
(CON) continues to be under discussion.

In sum, the state's more active involvement as a partner in improving the quality and reducing the cost appears to be producing results.

The Bad News

The "heavy lifting" — the expansion of health insurance coverage, with a few exceptions, has been stalled. Some additional funds have been captured to expand low income coverage to children and adults. However, the effort to share the cost in expanding coverage offered to small employers failed to garner the support necessary for legislative passage and Pennsylvania is now the state, next only to Michigan, with the largest losses in employer based coverage.

The Children's Health Insurance Plan (CHIP) and the state funded adult plan, designed for low income persons not eligible for Medicaid, have both been expanded with additional sources of funding. An expansion of the federal match to 68% has enabled an expansion of CHIP for those in families with incomes up to 300% of poverty or about one third more children. Families with incomes above 300% of the federal poverty level who cannot obtain affordable health coverage in the private market may purchase CHIP at state cost. A side benefit of this has been that many low income working families who applied for the CHIP program turned out to be eligible for Medicaid and the number of children covered by the Medicaid program increased. In addition a Community Health Reinvestment Agreement, negotiated with the state's four Blue Cross/ Blue Shield plans, has made available a proportion of their reserves — somewhat more than $100 million a year — to expand the adult Basic program enrollment. The AdultBasic program plan had originally been subsidized with tobacco settlement funds.[16]

---

[16] A 1998 master settlement agreement with the nation's tobacco industry ended further litigation against them for health damages in exchange for financial payments to the states participating in the agreement. The Commonwealth of Pennsylvania should receive a total of about $11.3 billion from this agreement spread over a 25 year period and currently receives about $400 million a year. In Fiscal Year 2007, $71 million of this was used to subsidize the adult Basic health insurance program for low income persons who do not qualify for Medical Assistance.

However, while an expansion of adult coverage was supported by the legislature, the Cover All Pennsylvanians bill which required extracting new funds from employers and the legislature died in 2008. In spite of a concerted effort by the Rendell Administration, it failed to get sufficient support for passage. In part it was victim of the Republican-Democratic ideological divide and a deteriorating economic environment that made both the legislature and the small business community more reluctant to absorb their share of the cost. A similar initiative in California met an identical fate (Curtis and Neuschler, 2009).

The Cover All Pennsylvanians bill was also a victim of the lobbying of special interests that perhaps poorly represented their members. The Rendell Administration had hoped to divide the small business community, appealing to the sense of fairness for small employers that provided coverage for their employees with a pay or play provision. (E.g. either you provide health insurance or we'll tax you and provide coverage for your employees through a state plan.) However, the Pennsylvania Chamber of Business and Industry which together with local Chambers forms a major lobbying force for small businesses mounted an effective campaign to defeat the bill. The National Federation of Independent Businesses (NFIB) also claimed part of the credit for the defeat. For the Pennsylvania Chamber of Business and Industry and the local Chambers, a major selling point in getting small businesses to pay their membership dues is the role they play in collectively negotiating health insurance plans for their member. Its insurance subsidiaries also provide the Chambers with an additional source of revenue. NFIB has a similar conflict of interest. The Cover All Pennsylvanians bill proposed a publicly subsidized plan for low income employer groups and this was viewed as a potential threat. Thus the "special interests" represented by the Chamber and NFIB were lobbying against the Governor's bill were their own insurance business' interests and not in the interests of their members.

The Hospital and Healthsystem Association of Pennsylvania also lobbied against the bill because of concerns that were probably not in the best interests of their members either. Some of the commercial plans that cover small businesses and plans that cover individuals pay hospitals well above what the larger commercial managed care and Blue Cross plans do. In the unlikely event that low income workers would purchase such commercial products on their own or that the number of small employers providing coverage through such plans would increase, the hospitals would lose the difference in what they would get paid. Of course, the more likely result would be that more would remain uninsured and the hospitals would not get any payment at all from them. The other reason that the hospital association lobbied against the bill was that a small portion of the disproportionate share payments that hospitals currently get from Medicaid would be shifted to help pay for the state's share of the cost of the plan. Disproportionate share payments go to hospitals that have a large share of Medicaid and uninsured payments to help compensate for care provided to the underinsured and the extra cost of caring for patients in a predominantly Medicaid service area. From the perspective of the state, it was a way of adjusting for the resulting decline in the uninsured. From the perspective of hospitals, it was taking money out of their pockets. On the balance, however, the hospitals probably lost revenue as a result of the defeat of the bill.

Could the opposition of the hospital association, Chamber and NFIB have been avoided and would it have made any difference? It is not clear whether this opposition was intractable or could have been overcome with minor design changes and added assurances.

It is clear, however, that the Governor's efforts to reform the health insurance industry will continue to meet stiff resistance from the health insurance lobby. Not surprisingly, insurance companies basically want no restrictions on the way they set premiums, the benefit packages they design or the profits they are able to make. The proposal to limit medical loss ratios (the proportion of premiums paid for health services) to no less than 85% has not been enacted. Efforts to standardize benefit packages so that individuals and small employer purchasers can compare plans and make informed choices have also been thwarted. There are still no significant restrictions on the rating factors that plans can use to set premiums giving them the opportunity to cherry pick low risk employer groups and leaving higher risk small employer groups with no possibility of obtaining affordable coverage. Pennsylvania is only one of two states in the country that has not limited rating factors and variations in premiums. Not surprisingly, the lobbyists for the health insurance industry hide these self-interests under the cover of an ideological battle that pits free market "solutions" against the costly "impediments" of intrusive government control and that it would "thwart" competition.

The ball in terms of expanding health insurance and reforming the health insurance industry is now in the Obama Administration's court. Its campaign proposals had many similarities to Prescription Pennsylvania plan. Indeed, Rendell was one of the names on the list to lead the federal healthcare reform initiative after the withdrawal of Obama's first choice for Secretary of Health and Human Services, Tom Daschle (Baker and Pear, 2009). Massachusetts' was the only state effort to develop a plan providing something close to universal coverage. The plan was largely shaped by the Heritage Foundation, a conservative think tank. The Massachusetts plan, as a consequence, placed greater weight on individual responsibility to obtain coverage and focused on increasing private market health insurance plan enrollment through public subsidies to make such coverage affordable to low income persons. Massachusetts is now struggling with the growing cost of the plan and its affordability.

Part of the problem in the passage of Cover All Pennsylvanians, as in all the efforts to achieve universal coverage, is a fundamental disagreement over the appropriate roles of government and the private sector in providing health insurance coverage. This is reflected in the Massachusetts plan. This ideological divide was even more starkly reflected in the differences between the McCain and Obama presidential campaign health insurance proposals (Andrulis, Smith *et al.*, 2008). Obama proposed establishing a new public plan with options similar to those available to federal employees, creating a National Health Insurance Exchange to enroll people in the public plan or purchase an approved private plan, income based subsidies for this coverage, and guaranteed eligibility regardless of pre-existing conditions. McCain's proposal guaranteed access to those with pre-existing conditions through a state run high risk pool run by private insurance companies that would establish "reasonable" premium levels. The Obama plan would provide federal income based subsidies for families to buy qualified plans and would also provide subsidies to employers to cover their catastrophic healthcare costs and to small employers offering health insurance. In contrast, the McCain plan would provide a refundable tax credit of up to $2,500 for individuals and $5,000 for families to purchase their own health insurance, and providing income related subsidies for that Guaranteed Access Program high risk insurance pools. Eliminating the employer provided health insurance exemption from individual income taxes and the availability of individual coverage would increase the likelihood that employers would drop coverage all together. For the McCain campaign, health insurance coverage would become exclusively a free market personal responsibility and for the Obama campaign, a mixed public and personal responsibility. The public costs for the original Obama plan would be $50 to $65 billion phased in with some of this arguably coming from savings in improved efficiencies and eliminating excessive subsidies to the private managed care Medicare Advantage plans supported by the Bush Administration and from discontinuing the tax cuts to those earning over $250,000 a year. The McCain campaign did not estimate the costs or sources of funding and emphasized that the focus would be on cost containment.

Just as with *Prescription Pennsylvania,* other differences in their plans related to controlling cost and improving quality seem relatively insignificant and amenable to compromise. With the limited success of health insurance reforms at the state level, the focus has again shifted to national level efforts to achieve universal coverage. In the approaches to expanding health insurance coverage as reflected in the campaign proposals, however, the battle lines have been drawn.

Final Postscript

> *Medicine is a social science, and politics is nothing else but med-*
> *icine on a larger scale. Medicine, as a social science, as the sci-*
> *ence of human beings, has the obligation to point out problems*
> *and to attempt their theoretical solution: the politician, the prac-*
> *tical anthropologist, must find the means for their actual solution.*

(Ashton, 2006)

What German doctor, scientist and public health activist Rudolf
Virchow observed more than a century ago still holds in the current struggle for something closer to universal coverage. Like the blind men and the
elephant, we grasp at different parts and, as a result, come up with different prescriptions. We can, however, learn from history, mistakes and a
growing appreciation of the complexity of the enterprise we are attempt-
ing to fix. The cases presented in this book attempt to stimulate such
learning.

As the examples in this book illustrate, the American healthcare system is complex but adaptable. We know a lot about how to make such
complex adaptive systems work (Plsek, 2001). The enforcement of a few
simple rules would help with the self-correction of its pathologies. In
brief, one could argue that the American healthcare system needs to be
placed inside, what one could call a "treatment triangle" (hopefully a non-
toxic one). This would involve taking very seriously three simple, overlapping and self-reinforcing principles:

1. *Transparency:* Transparency enables self correction. The lack of
   transparency allowed HealthEast (Case 1) to stray from its charitable mission, Allegheny Health, Education and Research Foundation
   (Case 2) to ignore the warning signs that resulted in bankruptcy, the
   Mobile Infirmary and healthcare system as a whole (Case 3) to
   avoid the accountability that could have ended racial disparities
   in treatment, and South Park Hospital and its non-profit parent
   (Case 4) to stray into a medically questionable, but profitable product line. The drive for transparency is reflected in the efforts of
   Prescription Pennsylvania (Case 15) efforts to reduce hospital

acquired infection rates and publicize the variations in prescription prices at pharmacies.

2. *Standardization:* Medicine and business require standardization in order to provide effective and efficient care to a population. A diagnosis, should lead to standard treatment. That treatment should be based on the weight of the medical evidence, not on who one is, where one is being treated or how much one is paying for the treatment. The pricing or payment system has to reinforce this standardization by assuring that profits and losses of providers are based on the care and not on whom they provide it to, what procedures they do or what insurance plans they accept. Franklin Maternity Hospital (Case 5) should not have gone bankrupt just because of a shift in payment incentives to acute-care hospitals. Fluctuations in nursing supply (Case 6) could be moderated greatly correcting the payment incentives to providers and staffing standards. U.S. Healthcare (Case 7) should not have been allowed to make up its own rules in terms of payment and benefits, selectively cherry picking providers and subscribers. HealthChoices (Case 8) could have been transformed into a standardized payment system for the entire regional population, passing on the savings and assuring a single standard of care for everyone. Prescription Pennsylvania's (Case 15) efforts to get standard infection control practices adopted in hospitals and interoperatability in the exchange of hospital electronic medical records reflect this drive for greater standardization.

3. *Solidarity:* What got lost in the transition to the modern American healthcare system and perhaps explains why it performs so much more poorly that the healthcare systems of other developed nations is the notion of social solidarity underlying the development of the earlier sickness funds — the notion that "we are all in this together." Concierge Medicine (Case 9) encourages a social class stratified system of care as do the "focused factories" described in Case 10. Other for-profit physician owned specialty hospitals that target privately insured patients arguably, reduce the quality of care for everyone, regardless of class. Only with the Gift of the Heart (Case 11) has there been a conscious effort to find an alternative method for allocating costly scarce resources. Certainly, the operation of Akhil Bansal's (Case 12)

internet pharmacy business and the inevitable cherry picking for Klaassen's Sunrise Senior Living operation (Case 13) illustrate the impact of the failure to heed the notion that we are all in this together, returning us to a period before early 20th century reforms. They illustrate the darker side of the further intrusion of the private enterprise system into the provision of care. The conventional wisdom concerning the appropriate roles of government and publicly traded corporations has changed significantly in the wake of the current financial crisis. Publicly traded corporations are legally treated as separate persons, making the actual persons that own them not fully liable for their behavior. This legal fiction, some argue, transforms corporations into the organizational equivalent of psychopaths (Bakan, 2004). Psychopaths are persons that should be carefully watched and certainly not trusted with the responsibility for our healthcare. Social solidarity, critical to the efficiency and effectiveness of health-care, at the very least, is an alien concept to a publicly traded corporation.

Certainly, as the Pottstown (Case 14) and the Rendell healthcare reform (Case 15) stories painfully illustrate, there are plenty of economic, political and ideological barriers that stand in the way of embracing the application of these three simple rules. Yet, one of the lessons of the history, mistakes and complexity embedded in all of these cases is that change is rarely incremental and that gridlock eventually bursts, producing profound and rapid change. The other lesson is that individuals and healthcare organizations have a remarkable ability to adapt to those changes. We can only hope that those changes bring out the very best in all of us.

> *We face the suffering of human beings*
> *Ground into gears of machines,*
> *That crushes the joy of nurturing life*
> *Pit pleas for help against privilege and price*
> *While we sleep fitfully in isolated routines*
> *May we soon awake to common dreams.*

> (*Smith and Kaluzny, 1975*)

About the Author

David Barton Smith is Research Professor in the Center for Health Equality and the Department of Health Management and Policy at the School of Public Health at Drexel University and Emeritus Professor in the Risk, Insurance and Healthcare Management Department in the Fox School of Business at Temple University. He has previously served as an IPA fellow in the Office of Research and Policy at the Center for Medicare and Medicaid Services and on the faculty of the Sloan Program in Healthcare Management at Cornell University and the Community Medicine Department at the University of Rochester. Professor Smith received his Ph.D. in Health Services Research from The University of Michigan. He was awarded a 1995 Robert Wood Johnson Health Policy Research Investigator Award for research on the history and legacy of the racial segregation of healthcare and continues to do research on this topic. He is the author or co-author of five books on the organization of health services, the most recent being, *Health Care Divided: Race and Healing a Nation* (The University of Michigan Press 1999), and *Reinventing Care: Assisted Living in New York City* (Vanderbilt University Press 2003). Professor Smith has authored or co-authored more than thirty-five health service research related journal articles including ones in *Health Affairs, the Milbank Quarterly and the Journal of Health Politics, Policy and Law*. He has also assisted health systems and community groups in all regions of the United States in conducting health and needs assessments. He currently teaches courses in managed care and public health management at

Drexel, serves as the Principal Investigator of a grant from the Robert Wood Johnson Foundation to assist in the evaluation of their public health initiatives and as a consultant to the Center for Gerontology and Healthcare Research at Brown University in the analysis of nursing home markets in the United States.

Bibliography

Abelson, R. (2004). Barred as Rivals, Doctors See Some Hospitals in Court. *New York Times*. New York City. April 13, Page C1.

Abramson, L. (1990). Healing Our Health System. New York, Grove Weidenfield. Agency for Healthcare Research and Quality. (July 24, 2006). "Obesity Surgery Complication Rates Higher Over Time: Press Release," Retrieved January 12, 2009, from http://www.ahrq.gov/news/press/pr2006/obessurgpr.htm.

Allen, K. G. (1999). Assisted Living: Quality of Care and Consumer Protection Issues in Four States. *GAO Reports*. Washington, Government Accountability Office.

America's Health Insurance Plans (2009). "About AHIP," Retrieved January 28, 2009, from http://www.ahip.org/content/default.aspx?bc=31.

American College of Surgeons (1920). "Hospital Standardization." *Surgery, Gynecology and Obstetrics* **30**: 641–647.

Andrulis, D., D. B. Smith, *et al.* (2008). Health Care Proposals of the 2008 Democratic and Republican Presidential Nominees: Implications for Improving Access, Affordability and Quality for America's Minorities. Washington DC, The Joint Center on Economic and Political Studies.

Angrisano, C., D. Farrell, *et al.* (2007). Accounting for the Cost of Health Care in the United States, McKinsey Global Institute.

Ashton, J. R. (2006). "Virchow Misquoted, Part-quoted and the Real McCoy." *Journal of Epidemiology and Community Health* **60**(8): 671.

Assisted Living Executive (April 2008). Largest Assisted Living Providers. Retrieved August 2, 2009, from http://www.alfa.org/images/alfa/PDFs/2008_Largest_Providers_ALE_magazine.pdf.

Avraham, R. and K. A. D. Camara (2007). "The Tragedy of the Human Commons." *Cardoza Law Review* **29**(2): 479–511.

Bakan, J. (2004). The Corporation: The Pathological Pursuit of Profit and Power. New York, Free Press.

Baker, P. and R. Pear (2009). A Nominee Trips, Health Care Drive Suffers Setback. *New York Times*. New York City. (November 4): A10.

Beck, E. C. (1979). "The Love Canal Tragedy." Retrieved September 11, 2009 from http://www.epa.gov/history/topics/lovecanal/01.htm.

Bhattacharjee, Y. (December 2008). "Caveat Donor: A Street Brawl in India Brings Down a Global Kidney-Transplant Ring." *Atlantic*: 29–30.

Bishop, G. (2007). Childbirth at a Crossroads in Southeastern Pennsylvania. Philadelphia, Maternity Care Coalition.

Bodenheimer, T. (2006). "The HMO Backlash — Righteous or Reactionary?" *New England Journal of Medicine* **335**(21): 1601–1604.

Brandt, E. (2005). OxyChem Closing Strictly Economic. *Pottstown Mercury*. Pottstown (January 6): 1.

Bredin, K., *et al.* (1995). "Decline in Quality of Life for Patients with Severe Dementia Following a Ward Merger." *International Journal of Geriatric Psychiatry* **10**(11): 967–973.

Burleigh, N. (2009). Secret Agent Depart. Whistle-Blower. *New Yorker.* New York City. (January 5): 20–21.

Burns, L. R., J. Cacciamani, *et al.* (2000). "The Fall of the House of AHERF: The Allegheny Bankruptcy." *Health Affairs* **19**(1), (Jan/Feb): 7–41.

Carnahan, S. J. (2006). "Does Concierge Medicine Promote Health Care Choice, or is it a Barrier to Access?" *Stanford Law and Policy Review* **17**(121).

Catlin, A., C. Cowan, *et al.* (2007). "National Health Spending in 2005: The Slowdown Continues." *Health Affairs* **26**(1): 142–153.

Center for Disease Control (2003). "Public Health and Aging: Trends in Aging — United States and Worldwide." *MMWR Weekly* **52**(6): 101–106.

Center for Disease Control (2009). Obesity: Halting the Epidemic by Making Health Easier: *At a Glance 2009*. National Center for Chronic Disease Prevention and Health Promotion. Retrieved August 2, 2009, from http://www.cdc.gov/NCCDPHP/publications/AAG/pdf/obesity_aaa.pdf.

Chapman, S. (1995). Interview. Philadelphia.

Christoffel, T. (1976). "Medical Care Evaluation: An Old New Idea." *Journal of Medical Education* **51**(2): 83–88.

City Paper (1989). "Death of a Birth Hospital" *City Paper* No. 235. (February 10–17): page 1.

Cobb, A. L. and H. G. Hotchkiss (2004). "AHERF: It May Have Started with a Bang, but Did it End in a Whimper?" *American Bankruptcy Institute Journal* **28**(8): 30.

Curtis, R. and E. Neuschler (2009). "Designing Health Insurance Market Constructs for Shared Responsibility: Insights from California." *Health Affairs* (Web Exclusive) 28(3): w431–w445.

Davis, K., C. Schoen, *et al.* (2007). Mirror, Mirror on the Wall: An International Update on the Comparative Performance of American Health Care. New York, Commonwealth Fund, May.

Department of Health Education and Welfare (1967). Title VI Decision Mobile Infirmary, Mobile Alabama, Part II.

Dilanian, K. and N. Phillips (2007). A Dysfunctional System; a Jumble of State-by-State Rules Let a Chain of Horrors Grow. *Philadelphia Inquirer.* Philadelphia. (February 26): A01.

Dylan, B. (1966). Stuck inside of Mobile with the Memphis Blues Again. Blond on Blond. Nashville, Tenn, Columbia Recording Studios.

Encinosa, W. E., D. M. Bernard, *et al.* (2005). "Use and Cost of Bariatric Surgery and Prescription Weight-Loss Medications." *Health Affairs* **24**(4): 1039–1046.

Fallis, D. S. (2004). Sites Woo Patients They Can't Protect: Some Ill-Equipped for Dementia Clients. *Washington Post.* Washington, DC. (May 24): A7.

Fitzpatrick, D. (2007). "AHERF's Ex-chief Bitter about His Fall." *Pittsburgh Post-Gazette.* Retrieved August 4, 2009, from http://www.post-gazette.com/pg/07308/831018-28.stm, DOI: November 4, 2007.

Flegal, K. M., M. D. Carroll, *et al.* (1998). "Overweight and Obesity in the United States: Prevalence and Trends, 1960–1994." *International Journal of Obesity* **22**(1): 39–47.

Fleishman, J. G. and A. Wlazelek (1987, January 18, 2009). "LVHC Isn't End of Pool's Dream," Retrieved August 4, 2009, from http://www.mcall.com/news/local/all-lvh-story-arc-083187-4,0,3640113.story.

Forbes (1997). "Compassion Pays." Retrieved August 4, 2009, from http://www.forbes.com/forbes/1997/0224/5904086a_2.html.

Friedman, S. B. e. a. (1995). "Increased Fall Rates in Nursing Home Residents after Relocation to a New Facility." *Journal of the American Geriatrics Society* **13**(11): 1237–1242.

Garlicki, D. (1990). Judge Urges HealthEast to End For Profit Business. July 13, 1990. Retrieved August 4, 2009, from http://www.mcall.com/news/local/all-lvh-story-arc-071390-1,0,1739559.story.

Government Accountability Office (2003). Specialty Hospitals: Geographic Location, Services Provided and Financial Performance. Washington, DC, U.S. General Accounting Office.

Government Accountability Office (2005). Physician Services: Concierge Care Characteristics and Considerations for Medicare. Washington, DC: 4.

Goldstein, A. (2001). Assisted Living: Helping Hand May Not Be Enough: Facilities Face Increasing Demands and Scrutiny. *Washington Post*. Washington DC. (February 19): 1.

Goldstein, J. (2006). Shrinking Waistlines, Growing Business; More are Turning to Surgery for Obesity, and a Bucks Hospital Profits. *Philadelphia Inquirer*. Philadelphia. (December 10): A01.

Goldstein, J. (2008). Drug Costs in a PA Dispute; Rendell Says the State Could Save Big on Medicaid Rebates. Companies, GOP Disagree. *Philadelphia Inquirer*. Philadelphia. (June 21): A01.

Goldstein, J. (2008). Philadelphia Transplant Programs Risk Losing U.S. Funds. *Philadelphia Inquirer*. Philadelphia. (November 29): A01.

Government Accountability Office (2006). General Hospitals: Operational and Clinical Changes Largely Unaffected by the Presence of Competing Specialty Hospitals. Washington, Government Accountability Office.

Governor's Office of Health Care Reform (2007). Prescription for Pennsylvanina: Right State, Right Plan, Right Now. Harrisburg, Governor's Office of Health Care Reform.

Gray, B. (2006). The Rise and Decline of the HMO. History and Health Policy: Putting the Past Back In. R. A. Stevens, C. E. Rosenbert and L. R. Burns. New Brunswick, Rutgers University Press: 309–340.

Greenwald, L., J. Cromwell, *et al.* "Specialty Versus Community Hospitals: Referrals, Quality and Community Benefits." *Health Affairs* **25**(1): 106–118.

Griffith, J. and K. R. White (2006). Community Health. The Well-Managed Healthcare Organization. Chicago, Health Administration Press: 341–380.

Herzlinger, R. (1997). Market Driven Health Care. Cambridge, MA, Perseus Books.

Herzlinger, R. (2006). Testimony by Regina E. Hertzlinger. Homeland Security and Government Affairs Committee. Washington, DC. (May 24) Retrieved August 4, 2009, from http://coburn.senate.gov/oversight/index.cfm?FuseAction=Files.View&FileStore_id=175e0ac6-29fb-45dd-8300-a7bc2ddf9320.

Himmelstein, *et al.* (2004). "Administrative Waste in the US Health Care System in 2003: The Costs to the Nation, The States and the District of Columbia, with State Specific Estimates of Potential Savings." *International Journal of Health Services* **34**(1): 79–86.

Hospital, S. H. (2009). "Sacred Heart Hospital Home Page," Retrieved August 15, 2008, from http://www.shh.org/about/default.asp.

Hurley, R. E., J. Zinn, *et al.* (1999). A Painful and Unproven Pursuit of Value. Philadelphia, Pew Charitable Trust.

Institute of Medicine (1996). Nursing Staff in Hospitals and Nursing Homes: Is it Adequate? Washington, D.C., National Academy Press.

Joel, B. (1982). Allentown. *The Nylon Curtain*, Columbia.

Kaiser Family Foundation (2008). "United States: Distribution of Certified Nursing Facilities by Ownership Type, 2007." *Kaiser State Health Facts*. Retrieved December 16, 2008, from http://www.statehealthfacts.org/profileind.jsp?ind=412&cat=8&rgn=1.

LaFlore, J. L. (1965). Letter to James Quigley, Assistant Secretary DHEW. Non-Partisan Voter's League Collection, University of Southern Alabama Archives. Mobile.

Lazo, A. (2009). Mclean Company May Seek Bankruptcy Protection.*Washington Post*. Washington, DC. March 3, page D01.

Leapfrog Group (2007). *Surgeon Volume*. Factsheet. Washington, DC, Leapfrog Group.

Leapfrog Group (2008). Evidence-Based Hospital Referral. Factsheet. Washington, DC, Leapfrog Group.

Lee, C. (2008). Physician-Owned Hospitals Faulty on Emergency Care. *Washington Post*. Washington, DC.

LeFlore, J. L. (1966). Letter to Robert Nash from J. L. LeFlore. *Nonpartisan Voter's League Collection,* University of Southern Alabama Archives.

Lehigh Valley Health Network (2008). Financial and Annual Reports. Retrieved January 18, 1009 from: http://www.lvh.org/downloads/ar-2008.pdf.

Lewin Group (2006). Medicaid Capitation Expansion's Potential Cost Savings. Washington, DC, Lewin Group.

Liu, J. H., D. S. Zingmond, *et al.* (2006). "Disparities in the Utilization of High-Volume Hospitals for Complex Surgery." *Journal of the American Medical Association* **296**(16): 1973–1980.

Longino, C. F. (1995). *Retirement Migration in America*. Houston, Vacation Publications.

Massey, S. (1999). "Anatomy of a Bankruptcy," Retrieved September 15, 2008, from http://www.post-gazette.com/aherf/.

MDVIP. (2008). "Are You Working Harder for the Same Money?" Retrieved January 6, 2009, from http://www.mdvip.com/NewCorpWebSite/Physicians/WorkingHarderSameMoney.aspx.

MDVIP. (2008). "MDVIP Corporate Fact Sheet," Retrieved January 7, 2009, from http://www.mdvip.com/NewCorpWebSite/AboutUs/AboutMDVIP/CorporateFactSheet.aspx.

MDVIP (2008). "MDVIP Establishes Committee on Cost Reduction Through Preventive Healthcare Chaired by Former Secretary of Health & Human Services Tommy G. Thompson." *MDVIP Issue Overview.* Retrieved January 5, 2008, 2009, from http://www.mdvip.com/NewCorpWebsite/AboutUs/AboutMDVIP/HealthIssuesOverview.aspx.

Mello, M. M., D. M. Student, *et al.* (2007). "Changes in Physician Supply and Scope of Practice During a Malpractice Crisis: Evidence from Pennsylvania." *Health Affairs* **26**(3): w425–w435.

Menacker, F. (2005). Trends in Caesarian Rates for First Births and Repeat Caesarian Rates for Low-Risk Women: United States, 1990–2003. *National Vital Statistics Reports.* Washington, DC, Center for Disease Control. **54**: 1–12.

Mobile Register (1966). Infirmary Has 100 Vacancies as HEW Stalls Medicare OK. *Mobile Register* (December 18): 1. Mobile.

Mobile Register (1966). Wallace Joins Protest Over Medicare Okay Denial. *Mobile Register* (December 21): 1. Mobile.

Mobile Register (1967). Mobile Physician Fatally Wounded. *Mobile Register*: 3, 6.

Mobile Register (1967). Mobile Physician Fatlly Wounded. *Mobile Register* (January 30): 1. Mobile.

Mobile Register (1968). Medicare, New Addition Top 67 Activities. *Mobile Register*: 1.

Morning Call (1990). Time for Courage in Hospital World. *Morning Call.* (July 15): 22. Allentown.

National Center for Health Statistics (1975). Selected Operating and Financial Characteristics of Nursing Homes in the United States 1973–74. *National Nursing Home Survey.* Washington, DC, National Center for Health Statistics: 10.

National Center for Health Statistics (2007). Health, United States. Hyattsville, MD.

National Center for Workforce Analysis (2004). Projected Supply, Demand and Shortages of Registerd Nurses: 2000–2010. Rockville, Bureau of Health Professions, Health Resources and Services Administration.

National Institutes of Health (2008). "NINDS Chronic Pain Information Page," Retrieved August 15, 2008, from http://www.ninds.nih.gov/disorders/chronic_pain/chronic_pain.htm.

Nicken, W. and E. Graves (2005). "Nursing and Patient Outcomes: It's Time for Healthcare Leadership to Respond." *Health Care Management Forum* **18**(1): 9–13.

Nixon, R. M. (1972). Annual Message to Congress on the State of the Union. Washington, DC, U.S. Congress.

Nursing Institute (2001). Who Will Care for Each of Us? America's Coming Health Care Labor Crisis. Chicago, University of Illinois: 1–31.

Obesityhelp (2009). "Hospital Profile — Barix Clinics," Retrieved August 4, 2009, from http://www.obesityhelp.com/morbidobesity/bariatric+hospital+detail+Barix+Clinics+fsh.html.

Organization for Economic Cooperation and Development (OECD) (2007). *Annual Report*. OECD. Paris, France.

Pennsylvania Economy League (1996). Greater Philadelphia Challenge: Capitalizing on Change in the Regional Health Care Economy. Philadelphia, Pennsylvania Economy League, Eastern Division.

Pennsylvania Health Care Cost Containment Council (2009). Hospital-Acquired Infections in Pennsylvania: Data Reporting in Period 2007. Harrisburg, Pennsylvania Health Care Cost Containment Council.

PHC4 (2009). "Financial Analysis Fiscal Year 07," Retrieved January 15, 2009, from http://www.phc4.org/.

Plsek, P. (2001). Redesigning Health Care with Insights from the Science of Complex Adaptive Systems. Crossing the Quality Chasm: A New Health System for the 21st Century. Committee on Quality Health Care in America. Washington, DC, Institute of Medicine: 309–322.

Pottstown Health and Wellness Foundation (2008). *Annual Report*. Pottstown, Pottstown Health and Wellness Foundation.

Pottstown Health and Wellness Foundation (2009). History and Goals. Retrieved February 14, 2009, from http://www.pottstownfoundation.org/pages/history-goals.htm.

Pristin, T. (2008). Debt Struggles and Elderly Living. *New York Times*. New York City. (November 26): 6. Retreived August 4, 2009, from http://www.nytimes.com/2008/11/26/business/26senior.html?pagewanted=1&_r=1.

Rand Corporation (2008). The Health Insurance Experiment: A Classic Rand Study Speaks to the Current Health Care Reform Debate. *Rand Health Research Highlights*. Santa Monica, Rand Corporation.

Riley, G. F. (2007). "Long Term Trends in the Concentration of Medicare Spending." *Health Affairs* **26**(1): 808–816.

Robertson, C., *et al.* (1995). "Relocation Mortality in Dementia: The Effects of a New Hospital." *International Journal of Geriatric Psychiatry* **6**(6): 520–525.

Robinson, J. (2004). "From Managed Care to Consumer Health Insurance: The Fall and Rise of Aetna." *Health Affairs* **23**(2): 43–55.

Rose, J. R. (2004). "A Caution Light for Concierge Practices." *Medical Economics* 81(10): 22.

Rosen, G. (1977). Contract or Lodge Practice and Its Influence on Medical Attitudes to Health Insurance. *American Journal of Public Health* **67**(4): 374–378.

Saxe, J. G. (1970). The Blind Men and the Elephant. The Illustrated Treasury of Poetry for Children. New York, Grosset & Dunlap: 232.

Schneider, A. and M. P. Flaherty (1985). The Challenge of a Miracle: Selling the Gift. *The Pittsburgh Press*. Pittsburgh, Pittsburgh Press.

Schubert, S. and T. C. Miller (2008). Where Bribery Was Just a Line Item. *New York Times*. New York City. (December 21): 1.

Schumpeter, J. A. (1975). Capitalism, Socialism and Democracy. New York, Harper.

Shiffman, J. (2007). "Drugnet," Retrieved August 4, 2009, from http://www.philly.com/inquirer/special/pill/.

Skiba, K. M. (2006). Mr. Thompson Goes Corporate: Former Governor Trades Washington for Whirlwind of Private Sector. *Milwaukee Journal Sentinel*. Milwaukee. (February 26): A1.

Smith, D. B. (1989). Editorial: Franklin Maternity is a great loss (February 6): A10.

Smith, D. B. (1999). Health Care Divided: Race and Healing a Nation. Ann Arbor, University of Michigan Press.

Smith, D. B. (2001). Long Term Care in Transition: The Regulation of Nursing Homes. Washington, D.C., Beard Books.

Smith, D. B. (2003). Reinventing Care: Assisted Living in New York City. Nashville, Vanderbilt University Press.

Smith, D. B. (2004). An Assessment of the Supply and Demand for Registered and Licensed Practical Nurses in the Commonwealth of Pennsylvania. Philadelphia, Department of Risk, Insurance and Healthcare Management, Temple University: 1–34.

Smith, D. B. (2004). A Health Assessment of the Pottstown Area. Philadelphia, Temple University.

Smith, D. B. and W. Aarronson (2003). "The Perils of Healthcare Workforce Forecasting: A Caste Study of the Philadelphia Metropolitan Area." *Journal of Healthcare Management* **48**(2): 99–11.

Smith, D. B., Z. Feng, *et al.* (2008). "Racial Disparities in Access to Long-Term Care: The Illusive Pursuit of Equity." *Journal of Health Politics, Policy and Law* **33**(5): 861–881.

Smith, D. B. and A. Kaluzny (1975). The White Labyrinth: Understanding the Organization of Health Care. Berkley, McCutchan Publications.

Smith, D. B. and J. Larson (1989). "The Impact of Learning on Cost: The Case of Heart Transplantation." *Hospital and Health Services Administration* **34**(1): 85–97.

Smith, D. B. and R. Pickard (1986). "Evaluation of the Impact of Medicare and Medicaid Prospective Payment on Utilization of Philadelphia Area Hospitals." *Health Services Research* **21**(4): 521–546.

Somers, H. and A. Somers (1961). Doctors, Patients and Health Insurance. Washington, DC, Brookings Institution.

Stahl, S. (2003). The Nation's Dumping Ground: 6 Area Landfills Take in the Most Trash in a State That is the Largest Importer. *The Mercury*. Pottstown (October 3): 1.

Stanton, M. W. (2004). Hospital Nurse Staffing and Quality of Care. Research in Action. Washington, DC, Agency for Healthcare Research and Quality.

Stark, K. and J. Goldstein (2003). Raising the Risk in Heart Surgery: New Programs, Shrinking Market Equal Safety Threat. *Philadelphia Inquirer*. Philadelphia (April 27): A1.

Stevenson, K. (April 29, 2007). "Stocks on the Fevered Fifty Publicly-Traded Nursing Home Companies Soar, then Crash," Retrieved December 22, 2008, from www.elderweb.com/home/node9708.

Stolz, R. (2007). "Have We Got a Deal for You; More Private Equity Firms are Turning an Eye Toward Small and Midsized Businesses." *SMB Finance Volume*, 2(6): 10.

Stone, C. (2008). The Impact of Hospital Ownership: Looking for Consistency Among Conflicting Findings. Findings Brief: Changes in Health Care Financing and Organization. Washington, DC Academy Health.

Stone, D. (1993). "The Struggle for the Soul of Health Insurance." *Journal of Health Politics, Policy and Law* 18(2): 287–318.

Task Force on Organ Transplantation (1986). Organ Transplantation: Issues and Recommendations. Washington, DC, Department of Health and Human Services.

The Hospital Association of Pennsylvania (2001). Pennsylvania Nurses: Meeting the Demand for Nursing Care in the 21st Century. Harrisburg, Hospital Association of Pennsylvania.

The Pew Health Professions Commission (1994). Physician Retraining as a Strategy to Enhance the Primary Care Workforce. San Francisco, University of California.

The Pew Health Professions Commission (1995). Health Professions Education and Managed Care: Challenges and Necessary Responses. San Francisco, University of California: 1–34.

The Pew Health Professions Commission (1995). Shifting Supply of Our Health Care Workforce: A Guide to Redirecting Federal Subsidy of Medical Education. San Francisco, University of California: 3–9.

Thorson, J. A. (1988). "Relocation of the Elderly: Some Implications for Research." *Gerontology Review* 1(1): 28–36.

Torregrossa, A. (2009). Interview with Director of the Governor's Office for Health Care Reform. Philadelphia (March 27).

USA Today (2004). Assisted Living Requires Aid: Closer State Supervision. (July 2): A10.

Wager, E. H., B. T. Austin, *et al.* (1996). "Organizing Care for Patients with Chronic Illness." *Milbank Quarterly* 74(4): 511–544.

Wu, W. and S. Machlin (2004). Examination of Skewed Health Expenditure Data from the Medical Expenditure Panel Survey (MEPS), Agency for Healthcare Research and Quality: 6.

Young, Q. (2007). Interview by author. (June 14). Chicago.

Young, R. K. (1990). In Re HealthEast, Inc. Orphan's Court Division of the Court of Common Pleas of Lehigh County 1988–1297: 285–302.

Young, R. K. (2006). Unsolicited Opinion: Regarding the Surplus of Revenue by the Lehigh Valley Hospital for 2005 of $75,000,0000. Allentown: 1–11.

Zipkin, A. (2005). The Concierge Doctor is Available (at a Price). *New York Times*. New York City (July 13). Retrieved August 4, 2009, from http://www.nytimes.com/2005/07/31/business/yourmoney/31docter.html?pagewanted=2&_r=2&sq&st=nyt&scp=1.

Zuger, A. (2005). For a Retainer, Lavish Care by 'Boutique Doctors'. *New York Times*. New York City (October 30). Retrieved August 4, 2009, from: http://www.nytimes.com/2005/10/30/health/30patient.html?sq=&st=nyt&scp=9&pagewanted=print.

Index